Instagram Marketing Algorithms

$10000/month business plan using your personal social media account- Learn how to take money online right now, how to build a brand and become an influencer

by

Leonard Carli Marketinglegacy

D0168387

Table of Content

Introduction

Who hasn't even heard of Instagram? No, actually, who don't have Instagram? This app, all of a sudden, has taken the world by storm, and it's easy to see why.

First of all, it's super easy to use – you don't have to be a tech genius to be able to use it and take advantage of its features to your full advantage. Secondly, society has slowly turned us into individuals who are obsessed with sharing pictures we like and the pictures of ourselves – we even added a new word to the dictionary to describe it: *selfie*.

May it be for the better or worse, we can all agree that our lives are run by technology.

Just take a look around, when you are in a public place, you would see how many people are glued on their phone, completely lost of awareness of what's going on around them. It has become a part of our lives that without it, we feel like we couldn't function perfectly.

Do you feel guilty about this? Don't.

We live in a different world now. So, you cannot compare our life to how it was a decade or two ago or the days before that. There were no smartphones back then. There were no apps that order us food, no apps that call us a taxi, no apps that show us what the weather is, and no apps that let us upload pictures of our dogs, our meal, and ourselves and get praised for doing so.

Today, there are many apps like Instagram that allow us to not only share pictures and videos but also let us communicate with friends and be aware of the current events. It's also so easy to get caught following the lives of our favorite celebrities or events being updated by people we follow on the platform. It's also so easy to spend hours on the Explore page watching cooking or dog videos.

Not any of these existed 15 years ago. Gone are the days we only had to rely on TV to get entertained. Now, we have Instagram to give us the same entertainment the TV gives us. With its convenience, it's not surprising why – we can now watch TV and get updated with the latest trends anytime and anywhere as long as we are connected to Wi-Fi.

This is why if you have a brand or business you want to sell, not having a dedicated Instagram account for it, means you're doing something wrong. Having an Instagram account is A MUST if you want your business to sell faster and thrive.

Instagram has a billion users on a daily basis and this number is continuously rising. This makes Instagram one, if not the best platform for marketing a business. Instagram has a spectacular reach and engagement that is about 60 times better Facebook and 120 times better than Twitter.

In this book, you will learn how to use this platform right, how your business can make the most of the features it offers, and how it changes the world of marketing.

Chapter 1: The Instagram world

Since 2010, Instagram has been proven to be the fastest-growing social media platform. But what makes this platform unique and effective? Well, what separates it from the rest is the creativity it offers.

Instagram has generated creative ways for users to share their content. For example, Instagram has allowed its users to share 10-second videos or photos on their account that disappears after 24 hours, it's meant to rival Snapchat and apparently, they won as more people prefer using it now rather than the original creator of the concept. The platform also allows users to show live videos that allow users to have real-time interactions with their followers – IG Live.

So, basically, their tactics just seem to always work and it gives so much advantage to people who want to market their business. The innovation it offers is one of the main reasons for its sudden, continuous boom.

Is it worth the fuss?

Instagram is the perfect app for sharing content via visual imagery. Generally, its audience is young, educated, and very into shopping. It has a different feel compared to platforms like Facebook and Twitter, with a focus on visuals rather than words. However, studies have shown that, like Facebook, it is used daily and makes for a loyal and highly active user base.

This ability to capture a younger, more creative audience is sounding the alarm bells for major companies who are looking to advertise on social media. With high usage, the increased interest in advertising on the app is not surprising. However, the competition is extreme so businesses will have to find creative ways to compete with their rivals in this visual haven of social media.

1.1 Knowing the Crowd of Instagram

Keeping yourself aware of Instagram's demographic is important in order for you to determine how you would get around in using this platform to your business' full advantage. This is important because by getting yourself familiar with the number, you will be able to plan your tactics better. This will prevent you from wasting your time creating content that will not work for the types of followers you might not have.

What you want is to invest your time in is presenting the applicable content for the right audience. On Instagram, because you are mostly using images and videos as the main content, you need to create images and graphics that are appropriate and captive to your following base. A great content strategy equals to good engagement.

Instagram demographics by age and gender

While there's still no way to know the specific demographics of your own followers, you may still want to know the general demographics of the entire platforms. Unsurprisingly, Instagram leans towards a much younger audience.

Here is the demographic for Instagram users:

- 13-17-year-olds – 72%

- 18-29-year-olds – 64%

- 30-49-year-olds – 40%

- 50-64-year-olds – 21%

- 65+-year-olds – 10%

Instagram demographics by gender

When it comes to gender, Instagram is more popular among females than males, but the difference is not that drastic. It shows that 50.3% of Instagram users are female, while the remaining 49.7% are male.

Instagram demographics by location

Although Instagram is available all over the world – except China, Iran, and North Korea – there are some countries that spend more time on it than the others.

A great way to manage your digital marketing strategy is to look at the statistics that show the usage of your target countries. When you know which countries use Instagram most, it's going to be easier for you to adapt and customize your content based on the audience going to be exposed to it.

With about 700 million monthly active users, the United States ranks number one when it comes to having the highest number of Instagram users and it's not really surprising.

However, despite having the largest Instagram active users, the United States has only a 34% penetration rate, which is lower compared to the highest penetration rate country, Aruba with a rate of 46% despite having only 4.7 million active users.

More than 80% of people who use Instagram are based outside the US, with some of the top countries including India, Brazil, India, and different countries in Europe.

Now, let's breakdown these users by region:

- users from urban areas – 42%

- users from suburban areas – 34%

- users from rural areas – 25%

How Fast Instagram is Growing

Instagram picks up new accounts faster than ever – especially since the app allows users to sign in up to 5 accounts in a single device. This gives users the ability to run their personal Instagram account along with their Instagram business accounts using a single phone.

As of this year, the platform gets about 1 billion monthly active users. And this number makes them the third most popular social media platform today – following Facebook with 2 billion monthly users and YouTube with 1.9 monthly active users.

The number of monthly active users is a commonly used metric with some sort of limitation. The figure doesn't allow for much nuance: a person who scrolls and posts to Instagram multiple times a day is way more important to the service than those who check in every once in a while. And growth for a certain period may include returning lapsed users, although that's not really that important.

Caveats aside, these numbers are definitely impressive. According to Instagram, the factors behind this continuous growth has something to do with its smart algorithm that allows users to easily find their interests easily. On top of it, the constant updates that add new features and improves the old ones make so much difference.

Chapter 2: Setting up Your Profile

One of the best things about Instagram is its ease of use. Creating an account and setting up your profile can all be done within 10 minutes. However, if you are creating an account to sell your business, you must put more thoughts and more time into it. In this chapter, let's talk about the *better* way to set up your profile that earns money.

First of all, you have to know that if you have an existing Instagram account, you can completely turn it into an account for your business. And because that existing account might be set as a personal account, you might have to change it into a business account. Turning your personal Instagram account into a business one will provide you with more features and settings beneficial for your business. These new features will help you reach more people and boost sales.

You have to keep in mind, however, that once you switched your business account, you will not be able to limit its privacy to only people who follow you. On top of it, you can only connect and share posts on a Facebook page associated with that new Instagram account. But then again, as mentioned earlier, because you can sign in up to 5 different accounts in a single app/device, you can always create a new one and still keep your personal account.

2.1 Coming Up with the Perfect Name

When it comes to creating an Instagram account, especially if it's for your business, the two most important components are your choice of name and username. This is because your potential clients or customers will search for certain keywords that might be relevant to what you offer.

When a user types a name or keyword in the search bar on Instagram, the app will only show accounts that have that use username containing the exact keyword typed, or at least the closest ones. For example, let's say your business is related to the Keto diet, then the people you want to attract are the ones who will search "keto diet" on their search bar. Meanwhile, Instagram will only show your account on the result page if your username contains those specific words. This means that if you want your account to show up on the result page, you may want to include the word "keto" or better, "keto diet" on your name.

2.1.1 Choosing the Username for Instagram

You are able to choose your username on the first part of setting up your account. An Instagram username is limited to 30 characters but when it comes to choosing a username, the simpler the username is, the better. Mainly because it makes your account easier to be tracked and remembered. Your username may only include letters, numbers, period, and underscore. Other symbols are not allowed.

Just like choosing a name for your account, you may want to pick a username that clearly represents your brand. It has to be recognizable and as much as possible describes what you do. However, with the number of competitions there is, your options now might be limited, so you have to be creative! It doesn't have to be exactly the same as the name of your business but make it as close as possible.

At the registration part of the Instagram account, you will be asked to create a username. If the username you choose is already taken, an X mark will show up then it will ask you to enter a new one. Otherwise, a √ mark will show up, then you'll be directed to the next step. Keep choosing alternatives until you get a username that is available for you to use.

Usernames are given on a first-come basis. If you use a desktop to create an account, you will be able to be given default suggestions by Instagram for ones that are still available containing the main keywords based on the name you entered as your business name or email address. You don't have to follow their suggestions, though. Especially that most of their suggestions sound spammy.

Again, if the initial usernames you want are not available, you can add periods or underscore. For example, if @kctodiet is already taken, you can use @keto.diet or @keto_diet. These will sound more professional compared to @ketodiet123. Unless your business name contains numbers, adding numbers to your username will make it sound unprofessional and may not be taken seriously. If periods and underscores don't work, you may also add words relevantly. For example, @ketodietUSA or other words that will still keep your name unique yet relevant. The added words could be your location base or something else.

After selecting a username, all the content linking to your profile should associate with the URL of your username. If ever in the future you want to change your username, your URL is also going to be changed, so you have to make sure to update all backlinks that are meant to direct to your Instagram account. This is why it's important that you choose the best one from the beginning because changing it later on when you already have a bigger following will involve so much work.

2.1.2 Choosing the Name for Instagram

Not only your choice of username is the only thing important for your profile. It's also very important to choose the best Instagram name. This name is what shows under your profile photo, the name that is in bold.

This is important because it gives you more opportunities to add more keywords to your Instagram account. You can use a name different from your username if you want. This is where you can use your creativity.

Unlike the username, your Instagram name doesn't have to be only one word. You can set it to anything you want and you can use any characters you want. However, like the username, you have a 30-character limit including the spaces you are going to use.

Usually, people use the name of their business as their Instagram name. This makes their profile look more well-set-up and more professional-looking.

The name you are going to use on your profile isn't going to be tied on your URL, so you can easily change it later on if you need to.

2.2 How to Set Your Bio that Generates Buyers

To write a bio for your Instagram profile might sound easy. After all, you can just write a couple of words and you are good to go. However, if you are running a business profile, you might want to put more effort into that.

You have to keep in mind that as a business, every detail is important and you must make the most of every feature available in marketing your business. Here are the tips that will help you put up an attention-grabbing bio...

Figure Out What You Want to Accomplish

So, what do you need to accomplish? This question is the first thing you need to answer before filling up your bio section. Here are some examples of goals you may come up with:

- To understand what your business offers

- To tell the audience how and when they can get in touch with you;

- To show the personality of your brand

- To inform the audience about your new products or services

- To prompt a call to action for your audience

Here is what you must always remember: Your business goal must appear in your bio.

How are you going to help your followers through your products or services?   This little section   in   your profile should help you sell yourself. Your profile may also include a link to your site or a specific product.

How long should the bio be – should it be short or long? The length of your bio all depends on the image and vision of your business. So, take your time and put that image and vision together and turn it into words if have not already.

Your bio must also go along with your overall social media tactics. How to do you write your captions? How do you compose messages on your Facebook posts and tweets?

Think of the words that you want to be associated with your brand along with the emotions you would like to carry with you. You can check out other brands' bio to get some inspiration, but make sure not to copy theirs!

Break it up

For some people, information that comes in smaller portions is easier to understand. So, to make it for everyone to understand, you may want to break up your bio using line spacing or the |. You can also add the following words or sentences on the next line. It seems to be more effective than writing it on the next line. It's also more common.

And here's a useful tip: Because typing directly on Instagram bio editing page doesn't allow you to add breaks, you can type your bio first on your phone's Notes app. When you're done, copy and paste it on your bio field.

Consider Adding Emojis

If you don't know already, about 50% of people who leave comments on Instagram posts use emojis. People just love it! And so, many brands take advantage of this fact!

Many people use emojis to express their emotions, especially when they want to sound friendly and approachable. On top of it, you can use it to break up your description easily. For example, you can use emoji instead of using the generic bullet points.

16

However, you must learn to use this carefully – you don't want to overkill it. Although many Instagram users love emoji, not everyone has the same feeling about it. Not everyone understands emojis the same way as others, so, make sure you are using the ones that are easier to interpret and remember that balance is everything.

Don't Forget the Hashtags

Hashtags basically run Instagram, which means if you want to be discovered, put them to good use! Did you know that 7 out of 10 hashtags used on Instagram are branded? If you don't know already, you can also use hashtags on your Instagram profile bio, not only on your individual posts. This will make your profile more discoverable. It's also a good idea to make your own unique hashtag/s dedicated to your brand. Something your clients can use when they want to post a picture related to your brand. Doing this can also help you collect feedback from your audience as well as photos from clients you can use as your own content.

Point Out the Link

Instagram doesn't let users add clickable links on photos or videos you upload on the platform – they only allow it on the bio section. Make the most of it! You can put that link just below the bio description, and so you want to highlight it. One of the most common and effective ways to do that is by adding pointing down emoji 👇 or the arrow down emoji ↓ just before the link.

Choose the Right Photo

If you are the brand yourself, then don't be afraid to use your own photo. Especially on Instagram, a profile that uses their own face gets 39% more likes. So, the profile photo you use definitely makes an impact.

But that's not only that – people would have more connections with brands using a face that looks friendly and more approachable. And when choosing a photo to use, it doesn't have to be too detailed as it's going to be small anyway, it just has to be clear and good quality. Try not to be too formal too – you don't use the same photo you would use on your LinkedIn profile. Make it a little bit casual, at least!

On the other hand, if you are running a business that doesn't revolve around your life, and is an actual company selling products, then a logo would be a better option. Using a logo as the profile picture for this kind of Instagram account is a better option for companies if they want their business to be remembered easily.

Bottomline

No matter how long or short your bio is, the important thing is that you take the opportunity to present and sell yourself and your products or services to your audience excellently. No matter what your goal is, it should always have to do with how you will be able to drive traffic to your site or products.

So, when making a bio, just take your time. It's worth it to spend some time crafting the perfect bio for your Instagram account. But then again, remember that there is no wrong way to create a bio. It's up to you how you want to write it – it can be serious, funny, short, or consume all the free 150-character limit. As long as it represents your brand, then you're good to go.

2.3 Creating Daily High-Quality Content in Ten Minutes a Day

The good thing about using Instagram to promote your brand is that making an engaging post doesn't have to consume a lot of your time in a day. Yes, 10 minutes is enough for you to work on what you are going to post on your business account.

While this might not be the case if you are just starting out, as you get to know how your followers respond to the contents you post, it is going to be easier over time.

As you probably already know, crafting high-quality, engaging content for your Instagram account is the most important part of growing your business on the platform. It's not hard to see the reason behind this – There is currently a huge competition on the world of Instagram and that is because of the huge presence the platform can give to businesses. You have to make yourself stand out. On top of it, the ever-changing algorithm Instagram put on the platform makes only high-quality posts be noticed.

This just means you need a great action plan and strategy to come up with like-worthy content. From taking the picture, editing it, and crafting the caption – you have to put an effort to make every post count.

But before that, let's talk about the Instagram algorithm because this is very important.

Changes in the algorithm on social media usually get a lot of bad rep as it makes it more difficult for businesses to adapt. However, these changes of algorithm don't stop anyone from growing, it simply changes the way your business grows. It also gives way for new accounts a chance to grow and make a name within the competitive world of Instagram. So, this could be good, especially for those accounts that are just starting out.

Aside from having high-quality content, consistency also counts a lot. No one really knows exactly how the Instagram algorithm works, but for some reason, there's a higher chance they push your posts to top if you upload on a regular basis, which means posting on regular basis means more exposure and more engagement.

When the algorithm sees that you are getting a lot of engagement, you'll have a better position on the newsfeed and even on the explore page.

But aside from helping you adapt more with the algorithm, posting high-quality content gives you the chance to actually monetize your account if you are an independent brand or sell your products or services if you are running an e-commerce page.

But then again, let's go back to the first important thing... Keep in mind that being able to learn how to craft high-quality content doesn't happen overnight. You need to exert some effort and creativity, and eventually, in no time, you will see how it pays off.

Here are 4 simple steps that will help you kickstart your content strategy for Instagram

Step 1: Set Up a Plan

There are two questions you must ask yourself before getting started.

- What kind of content are suitable for your brand?

- What kind of content does your audience want to see?

Knowing the answers to these two questions will make it easier for you to plan your content. It will be easier for you to craft content that will make an impact on people who will see it. You have to know that many Instagram accounts get sidetracked only because the content they are posting is irrelevant to the niche they have. So, the people who are following them get disappointed for not getting the content they expected, which can prevent their growth.

For example, if your niche is about food, then don't post anything related to jewelry. Also, many Instagram businesses, agree to collaborations, however, if the collaboration is no way relevant to your niche, posting posts from your sponsor may drive away your followers.

After answering these two important questions, planning ahead on what you are going to post for the entire week would be easier.

You can get started by listing down all the things you want to be on your page for the next 7 days, or longer if you can manage. For example, if you are a food-related account, then plan at least 4 recipes you can post, while the rest can be something else that is still relevant to your niche, like your favorite restaurants and/or cooking techniques.

So, this means that if you want to save time and spend only 10 minutes or less in a day creating captivating content, then you may want to take different photos in one batch. You can dedicate the Saturday to shoot photos and Sunday curating the caption for each photo you have taken the previous day. The more you organize your strategy, the easier you can pull this out, and of course, the more time you will be able to save.

Step 2: Take High-Quality Photos

If you really want to get serious on your Instagram business, then you need to invest in a good camera. It doesn't have to be a fancy DSLR, though. There are many smartphones that can take high-quality photos. After all, it's all about how you take the photos and not what you use to take it.

If you can't financially invest in a new gadget, then you might want to at least invest some of your time learning how to take better pictures. Learn how to take pictures from better angles and know more about lighting and composition. Use your creativity because of this what truly counts.

Don't be afraid to take as many photos as possible. This will give you better selections on which ones to upload. Not only you will have more selections, but you will also have more content to upload in the future, you will never run out. Also, thanks to the Instagram feature that allows you to upload multiple pictures in a post, you can take and upload photos at once without flooding the newsfeed of your followers.

Step 3: Edit Your Instagram Content

The world of photo sharing has suddenly changed, thanks to Instagram. As you can easily notice, most popular accounts with hundreds of thousands of followers have one thing in common – they have a consistent aesthetic they follow, usually the color scheme of their feed.

Following a consistent aesthetic is key to help your audience learn more about your brand. On top of that, giving them good photos is like giving them an eye candy that will make them keep coming back. Keep in mind that when a new prospective follower stumbles upon your profile, he can decide whether or not he wants to follow you within the first 5 seconds of browsing. So, if you want to give people a good first impression, then build an attractive profile.

And this has become achievable, thanks to editing apps and software. If before, only those who know how to use Adobe Photoshop are the ones capable of enhancing photos, anyone now can "create" images according to their preferences.

One of the most commonly used apps or software today is Adobe Lightroom. It is simpler than the intricate Adobe Photoshop but is enough to provide the users with the options to edit the color scheme of the photos. Another amazing thing about this software as well is that it has this thing called "presets."

Presets are the adjusted settings you can reapply to multiple pictures. This can really save you a lot of time. With just one click, you can keep consistency with your photos. They will look more professional and aesthetic. You can select from their readily available presets or you can create your own.

You can edit your pictures altogether in one day to save you even more time. Not only this will help you save time but this can also help you make sure that all photos look the same.

Step 4: Write the Caption

Now that you're done planning out your content, shot the right photos, and edited them according to the aesthetic you want, it's now time to post the photos!

But, before clicking the post button, you need to write an attention-grabbing, engaging caption. When you are running a personal Instagram account, it's so easy to copy and paste quotes online, but if you have a business account to run, you must optimize all the captions you will compose and post.

Have you ever wondered how those random accounts that leave comments on your posts that didn't follow you before found you? Well, those people are likely to have noticed your post from hashtags and geotags they follow with an intention to also make engagements. This is why adding captions, hashtags, and even locations on your posts are important and on top of this, this goes on your favor when it comes to improving your algorithm.

Your caption doesn't have to be too complicated – you just need a little bit of creativity. There are some keys to making a good caption. Those keys are the following:

- Write a draft first and review it. You can use your Notes app on your phone to do your drafts. If you're not sure about your draft, show it to your team members.

- If you are writing long, make sure to give them an idea on the first sentence on what you are talking about before the topic reaches 'Read More' - not everyone has the patience of reading long captions, so if you want to keep their attention, let the first sentences be straight to the point.

- Always use the relevant hashtags – you can add up to 30 hashtags, but you don't have to write too many hashtags. If you want the post to look cleaner, you can comment on the hashtags instead.

- Emojis wouldn't hurt.

- Include a Call-to-Action if needed.

By being dedicated and consistent with your niche and audience, and taking your time planning, shooting, editing, and writing your caption, seeing growth on your Instagram would be faster.

Chapter 3: Strategies in Engaging with your Audience

As you can tell from the previous chapter, uploading and sharing photos or videos on Instagram shouldn't be taken lightly if you are running your account as a business or influencer. But the work doesn't stop there! In order to make your content more effective, you need to make engagement with every post you make and to make posts that will initiate engagement.

When it comes to any social networking, engagement is the key. If you want to improve your presence and attract more followers, then this is a practice you need to master. So, in this chapter, we are focusing on the strategies you can follow to engage with your audience.

Leaving Comments on Brand That Are Within Your Niche

Let's start this chapter by talking about making engagement on other pages within your niche. Yes, you can make engagement outside your territory as long as the account or the post you are leaving a comment on is still within your niche.

When you leave a comment, make sure to add a personal touch by using the name of the owner of the account (Usually, it is located on their bio page, if not, use their username). Choose to leave the comments on accounts with the highest number of following. This is because posts from those accounts are more likely to be seen by many more users. You can also interact with other comments, as long as you're not claiming to be associated with the owner of the account.

When leaving a comment, avoid leaving one-word or just emoji comments. Make sure to read the post and leave valuable comments – it could be questions or some sort of appreciation. Make sure to not always leave the same comment or else, you might get reported as spam, which can leave your account banned.

3.1 How to Respond to Comments on Your Content

Responding to comments left in your content is as important as writing captions on your posts – it does wonder when it comes to the algorithm. Posts with many comments from different people are pushed up by Instagram.

Along with the Instagram algorithm, responding to the comments builds some sort of connection between you and your existing and potential followers. This can generate a positive impact on how they see your brand. These people are likely to feel appreciated and their loyalty to your brand will be stronger.

Here are some tips you can follow when it comes to responding to the comments being left on your posts:

Positive Feedback and Compliments

Getting positive feedback on your post is extremely good for your brand. For many, they would just tap the heart button to show that they like the comment and then move on with their day. There's nothing bad with that, but if you take your time to express gratitude, they will appreciate it more and they will be more than happy to leave you more comments in the future.

So, if you want to make someone appreciated for simply leaving a nice comment on your post, respond to it nicely. A simple "thank you" along with smiling emoji would make them feel like you are one of their friends and not some snob influencer.

Emoji-Only or Single-Word Comments

When someone left this kind of comment, you don't necessarily have to respond to them. But, if you're feeling gracious, as a simple "thank you" or tapping on the heart icon to like the comments would be enough.

Rude or Negative Feedback

Unfortunately, many people still find the need to say something bad on the internet. Instead of expressing their disappointment in a better manner, they choose to lash out and leave hateful comments. When this happens, you can handle this by letting it go and flagging the comment as abusive content.

Remember that it's important for you to keep a good positive image of you for your brand, and engaging with these kinds of people will not help your brand grow, instead, it might even dent it.

As for negative feedback or complaints on your product or service, always keep your professionalism by responding nicely, even if they are cussing – they might not be happy with your service that's why they are angry, and that's okay. Ask them to send you a Direct Message so you can discuss the problem privately. Always keep your calm and don't fight negative comments with aggression. If you need some time to think of what to reply, that's even better. Take your time – take a deep breathe and respond with respect.

Questions

Most of the time, people would ask inquiries about your products, services, or promotions you announced on your Instagram post. You have to be quick in responding to this kind of questions as they might actually want to make transactions with you.

If you want to save some time and actually reply to your potential clients quickly, then you may want to prepare templated answers to the most commonly asked questions. For example, they might ask how they can contact you, type a response to this question on your Notes app and save it. Then when someone asks the same question, you can simply copy that and paste to the comment as a reply. You'll save so much time!

If the question happens to require a longer answer, then encourage the user to send you a Direct Message. Or better yet, send them a message directly, and then reply to their comment saying that you responded to their inquiry via direct message.

Spam and Tags/Mentions

Unfortunately, Instagram still doesn't have full control over spam accounts, and any public Instagram account probably has experienced being mentioned by a spam account. You can simply delete the comment if you don't want them on your post and then report them to Instagram. It's easy to tell whether or not an account is a spam account. The first sign is that they have only a single or no post. They also usually use pictures of sexy women in skimpy clothes or bikini.

As much as it is crucial to update your Instagram account with new posts in order to gain more followers, it's also important to constantly check back into those posts and respond to the comments as soon as possible. This will keep the engagement going. This delivers a positive message to your followers and will push you up on top of the Instagram algorithm. By keeping your engagement game strong, you are working your business' way to the top.

3.2 How to Run a Contest on Instagram

One of the most effective ways to attract new followers and brand recognition is through running a contest on your Instagram. Seriously, if done correctly, you can gain at least 1000 new followers by the end of the contest period.

But is it really worth it? What if you're just starting out on your business? Keep on reading.

3.2.1 Reasons to Run a Contest

Well, no matter how new or old you are in this scene, the answer would always be a YES! Here are some reasons why you should consider running a contest on your Instagram account:

- **Raise Brand Awareness Through the Platform**

In social media, visibility is EVERYTHING. And there's no doubt that running an Instagram contest is one of the fastest ways to get your name out there! Who doesn't love winning free stuff? Your followers will have no problem tagging their friends and family just to have a higher chance to win your contest.

And with this tagging, the ultimate domino effect will take place. Before you know it, everyone who has been tagged will also start tagging and the newly tagged ones will do the same thing and the same thing will happen over and over. And of course, those people tagged and are tagging are likely to follow you to get a track of who's going to win.

- **Boost the Engagement**

When running a contest, get ready to receive tons of notification – it will blow up your phone. You will get flooded with likes and comments. But the Instagram algorithm will love you because of this! You will be shown to more people on Instagram that it thinks will be interested in your contest.

- **Drive New Followers**

If you want guaranteed new followers, then run a contest that requires the participant to follow you before they gain entry to the contest. But then again, even without requiring this, they are still likely to follow you because they want to keep updated with who's going to win in the contest.

3.2.2 Different Types of Contests You Can Run on Instagram

Okay, so by now you've probably convinced that running a contest on Instagram is a brilliant idea. Now let's talk about the different types of contests you can have.

1. Photo Challenge Contest

This is one of the most popular types of Instagram contests. This involved making participants to upload photos on their account, tagging you, and using specific hashtags for that contest. You can also get them to mention your name in the caption and tagging other

friends. This is a good contest that brings domino effect –
now that you are mentioned in their post, your name and
contest are getting exposure.

2. Repost-to-Win Contest

Just like the photo uploading contest, this one also
involves requiring your followers to post pictures on their
personal accounts but in this case, they have to take a
screenshot of a specific photo you want them to upload.
This photo usually includes your branding as well as the
contest details in order for other people to see what's going
on. Again, don't forget to require them adding specific
hashtags and to tag you.

3. Like-to-Win Contest

This is the easiest contest to run, and probably the one
that gets most participants. This might not get you a lot of
new followers but it boosts your place in the algorithm
game, more importantly, you're making many of your
followers happy.

4. Comment-to-Win Contest

Like the previous one mentioned, this one is many
people's favorite because it requires a minimal effort – just
to leave a comment on your post. This can be as simple as
asking what they love about your product or service or
about something else relevant to your niche or something
more creative like giving a caption to your photo. There
should be endless ideas! Make sure to limit them to one
comment per account, otherwise, your post might get
flooded with comments from a single user.

5. Tag-to-Win Contest

This is something becoming the most popular Instagram contest today. In this contest, the users that want to join are required to tag some of their friends (usually 3 to 5 friends who are on Instagram) and convince them to join as well and follow your page. And before you know it, you're gaining new followers and more engagement.

6. Follow-Me Contest

Now, the last but not the least is the simple follow-me contest, which definitely is the best way to gain new followers and of course, boost your brand awareness. You can do a combination of any methods of any of the contests mentioned above like having to tag other people, liking your post, or commenting on it, along with having to follow you. Using a mixture of the entry methods above PLUS requiring anyone who wants to enter the contest to follow you. This would be a good way to improve your Instagram account and presence.

3.3 How to Partner with Influencers

Instagram influencers are basically the people who are making it to the top of at social media game. They're considered innovators and experts in this field. They are constantly chosen to be brand advocates due to their strong credibility and wide-ranging reach with a certain audience.

If you want to have leverage in the game, then partner with the right influencer that will truly help your brand. By choosing the right person to partner with, you will have the ability to draw a bigger audience. And to help you do that, here are the important step to finding and reaching out to the right influencer to partner with.

Set a Goal

When partnering with an influencer, it's important to build clear goals or objectives for the strategy you want to execute. Some of the common goals you might have in mind include:

- To boost engagement

- To increase credibility and brand awareness

- To extend the reach of the uploaded content

- To increase brand awareness and credibility

- To gain more followers

You can set the SMART method in setting your goals.

Specific

Measurable

Attainable

Realistic

Timely

One of the biggest mistakes you can make is reaching out to an influencer and asking them to make a collaboration with you without a proper plan. You'd be super lucky if you ever get a reply! If you want to be more successful, make sure that you are prepared – do homework, and define your SMART goal. It's important that you explain to them clearly what your intentions are and why you are doing it.

For example, if you are running an account with a niche related to cooking, you can collaborate with a chef influencer and show your interest in wanting to post one of their recipes on your account. As you do so, you have to provide them good information on how they can benefit from it. You need to propose them irresistible offers that would make them hard to say no to.

Regardless of what your reason is for asking them to collaborate with you, it's extremely important that you can tell them what you want to happen exactly. So, make sure that in the proposal you are going to write – which we are going to talk further later on – you tell them what you want, how you want it to be done, and how they can benefit from it.

Learn from Existing Brands

For first-timers, the best place to get started is to do research about your competitions and how they work things out. You can also monitor just any account within your niche but outside your demographics. Study the kind of content they post to see which content gain the highest level of engagement.

Generate a Plan of Action

Coming up with a plan of action is the next crucial thing you need to do. When generating a plan of action, you can start with a brief and tangible goal. This will allow you to have a particular target and help the influencer learn further what you really want.

You're the one to decide which goal suits better with your business and marketing tactics. Even though it's very important to have an action plan, you should allow your influencer to do their own thing and use their creativity. Don't try to control them and limit them in expressing themselves. You want their message to be authentic.

Identify the Best Influencer for Your Brand

When searching for the right influencer for your brand, it's important for you to be aware of the desires, goals, aspirations, and fears your customers share. By making yourself aware of this information, you will easily determine the most influential people for your followers and targeted audience. Keep in mind that influence is not equal to popularity. Remember that followers can be bots and bought – not because someone has a huge following, it doesn't mean that you can benefit from them 100%.

When searching and choosing for influencers, here are three important Rs you need to focus on:

Reach: These stats reveal the size of the audience of the influencers. This will be the number of followers, average likes, and comments.

Resonance: This will tell you how the followers interact with the content of the influencer uploads. This is the number of comments, likes, and shares.

Relevance: This will tell you how relevant their niche is to yours. This would be the hashtags and keywords used whenever the influencer makes a post.

By checking out the influencers' reach, resonance, and relevance, you will be able to know more about their impact on the community and how and if they can truly benefit your brand. Just like a real-life relationship, it's important to make some sort of connection or rapport with them before making any form of deal with them. You can start making connections with influencers by interacting with them as a follower.

Leave nice comments and like their posts, maybe share their contents, then, later on, reach out via DM. By doing this right and in a consistent manner, connecting and collaborating with influencers will be easier.

Build Real Relationships with Influencers

At this point, you should know which influencers you might want to reach out to and what you are going to tell them derived from your goals, what the next question is, and how are you going to approach them. Should you slide them a DM? Should you email them? How about the pitch, how would you compose it?

Here are some tips that can help you put things together

- **Think like the Influencer**

Put yourself in the influencer's shoes. Think of what their priorities are and what their goals could be. The area they are in and what interests them. When collaborating with the influencers that you want, let them know the reason why you are approaching them and how and if they can really make a difference to your campaign.

- **Show What You Have to Offer**

When it comes to offering values, you must also have something to put on the table. If you can benefit from the other brand as well, then you'll have a higher chance to get the collaboration. Otherwise, it's a shoot for the moon, unless you are willing to pay the influencer to do the collaboration. If you are uncertain, there's nothing wrong with asking them what you could do for them and what kind of leverage they may possibly be looking for to make them agree with the collaboration.

You can also send them some of your products as a gift — they can even give your products free reviews (which can also drive you traffic) if they're feeling generous in return for your generosity. But in the end, what you want is to make them agree to collaborate with you.

- **Make Relevant Offers**

Keep in mind that the demand of your market is not the only thing that is important, but also what the influencer wants. If your niche aligns with the interests and values of the influencers, they'll be more interested in engaging with your campaign and they'll be more invested in the partnership you are trying to offer.

Keep in mind that the influencers you are reaching out to are also people with hobbies and passion. If you figure out their interests, it's going to be easier for them to figure out how they can contribute to your campaign and get successful results.

By letting the influencers align their passions with your brand, it will generally lead to a more invested partner who is more motivated in promoting your brand and/or the product you are trying to offer.

3.3.1 How to Make the Perfect Pitch for Collaboration

Making the perfect pitch is the key to convincing the influencer to agree to collaborate with you. A pitch is meant to pinpoint the information that is relevant and valuable for the influencer's decision-making.

A pitch should be professionally but lightheartedly written but more importantly, genuine and straight to the point. Here is a template you can follow:

Hi, [Name of the Influencer]!

I am [Your name] from [Your company]. I've been following your account for a while - [Talk about what convinced you to follow them and what you like about what they post].

I am sending this message to you to ask if you'd be interested in partnering with us for a [The concept goes here, e.g. product review, contest, etc.]

We offer [Write what you offer to the influencer here, e.g. monetary payment, free products, etc.]

It's up to you how you want to present the content - your unique outlook is what we are eager to have.

If you're interested, can we set up a call to discuss this further?

I hope to hear from you!

Best,

[Your name]

Of course, you can customize this mail according to your preference. Just make sure you offer relevant, genuine information.

Do the Hard Work

Do the hard work – your influencer is not your staff. As much as possible, you want to make it easy for your new partner to carry out the job. For example, if the influencer needs to know more details about the product involved, get resources ready for them. If you want them to say something more specific about the product, let them know exactly how you want it to be written (this is usually applicable for those who are paid to do the collaboration).

They might make some modifications, but it's going to be better for them if they don't have to do it from scratch.

Make a Decision on How the Partnership Works

Again, once you have found the best influencer to collaborate with, you must have an agreement that can benefit both of you. And here are the most important aspects you have to focus on:

Content: Both parties should agree on the type of content that will be created for your brand. This means that even though you agreed that the influencer has the right to say anything he or she wants, it still has to have your approval. For example, you have to make sure that the information being shared is accurate or the link included is written correctly.

Time: Don't forget to set a specific deadline on when you need the content to be published and the influencer must agree to it.

Rights & Ownership: Create an agreement about content usage rights. In general, the content creator (the influencer) has every right to that content, however, they still have to have your permission if they want to share it somewhere else other than their Instagram. They also can't hold ownership of the brand and must declare that it's only a collaboration (only if that's what you want).

Retribution: Clarify the payment method, dates, and amount that you agree to pay even before starting the project. You can always negotiate or even get a free service in exchange for something else – like doing the same thing for them on your own account or free products or services. But then again, if they refuse to accept the offer unless it's paid monetarily, you must respect that. Keep in mind that it took them a lot of time and a lot of hard work before they got to the point where they currently are.

Hashtag use: You have to know that there are different regulations when it comes to sponsored content, and they change all the time. However, it's important that the influencer is using the hashtags #spon or #ad in your campaign. This will tell the people who will see it that the post is a sponsored post.

Chapter 4: Turning your Followers to Become Customers

Social media is without a doubt an essential component of a successful digital marketing strategy. It's one of the best mediums to boost your brand's awareness and reputation online — where first impressions are important.

More likes, shares, and followers are all great for your online reputation, but social media can provide your business with more valuable things than that. This is why small businesses are doing their best to make a name on social media as it's possible to convert follows into new customers.

However, it takes strategic planning and persistence to get more customers from your social media marketing. This chapter will talk about that.

4.1 Using Promo Codes

Who doesn't like a discount? Giving away promo codes to your followers is one of the best ways to turn your followers into clients. The benefits of doing it on your Instagram is that it doesn't require the follower an effort to get the promo code, it's easily available to them by just scrolling and remembering the codes written. You can also add a link that initiates a call to action to your followers – this link leads them to the website where the code is going to be automatically used.

Popular Ways of Sharing Discount Coupons on Instagram

There are several ways for you to share the discount codes successfully. Here are those ways:

If you would like to give away a promo code during a special holiday, then design your coupon with images related to this occasion. Add texts to the image, stating the value of the coupon along with instructions on how to redeem it. You can put the code in the photo, however, it is necessary that the discount is clearly shown in it. Also, don't forget to write the date validity in the description as well as the terms of use.

If you want to take it to the next level, you can even create a video to distribute the promo code. The success of this campaign heavily depends on your creativity.

If the promo code you are giving away is only valid for 24 hours, then posting on your Story would be the perfect option. This way of giving away coupon code is the most popular way used by companies today.

Most active Instagram users upload and watch stories every so often – it really replaced Snapchat today. This has become a favorite feature of people who keep certain aesthetic on their Instagram account as they don't need to spend more time taking multiple pictures and edit them just to pick the best one to upload as the posts disappear after 24hours anyway (unless you put them in the Highlights).

Chapter 5: Instagram Marketing

The world of Instagram has made it a lot easier to take and share pictures with the world in a more fun and fulfilling way. Besides networking, you can efficiently use Instagram for marketing. Instagram is an amazing promotional tool you are able to use to promote your business on the internet.

Instagram Advertising Overview

When it comes to Instagram advertising, this specifically referred to paid posts within the app. Promoting on social media with the use of organic campaigns might seem counterintuitive, but you know what they say: you have to spend money to earn money. And in the end, you will see how Instagram ads can really bring in unmatched results.

As of late December 2018, Instagram received 800 million active users who have shared 300 million stories. About 25 million of those are businesses that are vying for the same prospects your business is. However, these posts are only made to be visited naturally to be followers who stumble upon them.

If you want to take it extra further, then you should consider paid advertising. This will get your posts directly to people's faces who would otherwise never see them – whether it's due to the fact that they follow you or they happen now to be online when you posted them, or they just follow too many people to even get to your story. Paying Instagram to put your post in the first line will give you more exposure. You have control who will see them and how long you want them to be seen.

Using a visual medium to advertise is one of the most effective way of catching people's attention – they would rather spend time looking at pictures and a few largely written words to understand the message rather than read lengthy article just to learn about your promotional sale, that's why Instagram is very effective for many businesses.

Generally, using Instagram to promote business-related announcements is not too different from posting personal Instagram posts – you choose a picture to upload, edit it to the way your followers will understand the message, and upload it! This whole process will allow you to upload your ads to fit flawlessly into your profile. When your followers see these ads, they wouldn't feel like you are shoving your ads to their face – they will feel like it's just another post by an Instagram account they are following.

Introducing Your Products or Services Using Photos and Videos

They always say that photos worth a thousand words, and Instagram is all about expressing ourselves, our feelings, and memories through photos. But if you're someone running an Instagram account for business purposes, then you know that it doesn't work the same as it would if it was a personal Instagram account. You need to post pictures or videos of your products that wouldn't look annoying to your followers – you need to put effort to make it likable and relatable to your audience. And at the same time, your main intentions should still be to boost awareness for your brands in the hope to increase your sales. It doesn't mean the pictures or videos have to do professionally. The most important thing is that it's going to highlight the main features of the products or goods you are trying to sell. Make sure that the ads you are creating show the best of what you have to offer.

Today, it seems like more marketers are fond of using Instagram video features to promote their products rather than simple pictures. This is because it can deliver a clearer message and with a touch of creativity, it can be extremely entertaining to your followers.

5.1 Planning an Ad Campaign on Instagram

While Instagram is yet to beat the number of daily active users on Facebook, there's no denying the fact that they are winning when it comes to ad effectiveness. However, this would only work if you know how to run them. Maintaining an Instagram active presence is one of the best ways to do it. You must also know how to make the most of the advertising features offered by the platform. The following are the ways how you can manage an ad campaign on Instagram account.

5.1.1 How Instagram and Facebook Incorporate

When Instagram started, it was a 13-person start-up. The platform became popular quickly, though, and big companies took notice. The app ultimately sold to Facebook for $1 billion.

This union with Facebook is good news for advertisers. Facebook now allows you to run your Instagram advertising campaigns through the same dashboard that you use for managing your advertising on Facebook. The Ads Manager works exactly the same for both social networks once you have set up and connected your Instagram account.

5.1.2 How to Get Started with Your First Instagram Advertising Campaign

In creating your first Instagram ads, the first thing you need to do is to connect your business' Facebook page to your Instagram account. Yes, since Facebook bought Instagram for $1 billion, a strong union was built allowing Instagram users to manage their ads through Facebook. So, if you don't have a Facebook page set up for your business, then you MUST create one, otherwise, you would not be able to set up a business account on Instagram. You can create a Facebook page using your personal Facebook account, just log in and find the option for creating a Facebook page.

Once you successfully integrated your Facebook page account to your Instagram page, you can then start adding general contact information about your business which are the email address and phone number. If this information is included on your Facebook page, then it's going to be set on your Instagram by default. Not only you need a Facebook page to create an Instagram account for your business, but it's also necessary to run ads on the platform.

After setting up everything, you are ready to start managing the ads. You can do that by signing on Facebook Business Manager account and then add your Instagram account to an existing Business Manager account. Go to Business Manager>Business Settings>Instagram Accounts. From there, follow the cues that direct you to claim your new Instagram account and connect it with your marketing.

In the Ads Manager, just click "Create." From there, you can choose from Guided Creation or Quick Creation. If it's your first ad, then we'd recommend for you to choose Guided Creation as this is going to be easier for you to handle the ads on the process of generating an Instagram advertising campaign.

You can get started with the Guided Creation by choosing an objective for your campaign. This will you tell what you want to accomplish by putting your ads on Instagram. Is it to boost your brand awareness? Perhaps to drive traffic to your site? Do you just want more views on your videos? Or maybe turn your followers to clients?

5.1.3 Five Types of Instagram Advertising Campaign

There are four basic types of Instagram ads, each of which has its own characteristics. Here are those 5 types.

1. Photo Ad

Doing the advertisement using a photo is probably the least complicated way to make an ad, after all, Instagram is mainly made for uploading photos. When making a photo ad on Instagram, you must upload images that talking positively about your brand – it has to be powerful and relatable. These are effective in making the campaign as it doesn't require your followers to perform any action – they just have to scroll, look at the photo, and hopefully follow the call-to-action. And with that few seconds of them staring at the pictures, they're likely to have the knowledge and good impression about your brand.

2. Video Ad

A video ad on Instagram can go up to 60 seconds long. But then again, you don't need 60 seconds to grab people's attention – the first 30 seconds are the most important, so make the best of them. It's extremely important that you make engagement with your viewer immediately as soon as the video starts. Otherwise, they're likely to ignore your post and continue to scroll down. This kind of ad is amazing for brands whose products are just starting out. The video has the ability to be more captivating compared to the image.

3. Carousel Ad

Carousel ads a newer feature of Instagram which allows users to upload multiple pictures. And for business owners, this is a good way for them to upload a line of photos to showcase their multiple products or a single product from different angles. For example, if you are selling makeups, you can upload swatches of lipstick you are selling on different skin complexions.

4. Story Ad

An even newer feature, and also more used way of advertising, Instagram Stories allows the business owner to upload photos or videos of their products, without the need to spend hours taking and editing the media as it only shows up on the feed for 24 hours. As mentioned earlier, there are many reasons why Stories are every effective, but one of the top reasons is because more people can see it.

So, how does this feature help businesses turn their followers into new clients?

Even though pictures and videos on Stories only last for only 24 hours, they bring a lot of benefits. Actually, it seems like more Instagram users are more interested to watch Instagram stories than scrolling on newly uploaded photos – one of the main reasons for this is because posts on this feature are more personal.

Another reason why more businesses would rather post their ad campaigns in their Stories is that it's less likely to miss a post on Stories rather than on the newsfeed. It's easier for Instagrammers to watch stories than to scroll down their feed for new posts.

This is very beneficial to those who haven't gotten around the algorithm game just yet and want to deliver the message clearly to their audience. Another good thing about this is that adding tags and geolocation on the Story posts can be highlighted easier, making followers more aware of the message.

When it comes to introducing a product, you can take advantage of the fact that this feature allows you to portray the products you are selling from different angles in a more detailed description – more than you could do when you do it on a regular Instagram post.

You can also use this to promote testimonial. An effective way to promote and sell your business is to gather all the testimonials from your previous clients. Don't waste the comments and remarks that speak positively about your business! You can take screenshots of these comments (even if it's from Instagram or Twitter) and make a Story Highlight titled "Testimonial" on your Instagram page.

You can also repost some of the Stories from other users that mentioned your page to express their positive comments about your service or product. When your followers see that you post them and give them exposure on your Stories, they might also be interested to get featured so they will also post the products or services they purchased from you. When your followers see that many people trust you through these testimonials, then you will get more sales.

These testimonials are also a good way to show your clients that you listen to them and you appreciate them. That your priority is their satisfaction.

There are approximately 150 million Instagram users watch stories feed on a daily basis. Because stories feature content that disappears after only 24 hours, people are more intrigued about them. On top of that, tapping the screen is easier than scrolling down.

In the current algorithm, Instagram put posts that are getting the most engagement to the top. On the other hand, Instagram stories show the ones you haven't seen yet.

5. IGTV Ad

IGTV was launched in mid-2018, and many influencers and businesses definitely put this new feature to good used. Based on what its features show, IGTV is meant to compete with YouTube.

Similar to turning your television, IGTV plays videos as soon as you get on the IGTV tab. You don't need to search for a specific video to watch. You will be automatically shown videos based on who you follow and the content you like. To discover more videos, you can simply swipe to browse through. Viewers can also leave comments and like the video if they want.

So, how is this beneficial for businesses?

Well, because IGTV shows the videos vertically or in portrait mode, there's less pressure for the creator to produce professional videos. This is perfect for businesses who want to create videos similar to Stories, but want to keep them long and for them to stay in the platform for longer than 24 hours.

The kind of videos that are perfect for IGTV includes product unboxing, tutorials, product demos, tours, BTS, and other instructive videos relevant to the company's niche.

5.2 Best Practices on Instagram Ads

For a time, Instagram only allowed its users to upload square pictures with a ratio of 1:1. Today, however, Instagram has allowed users to upload photos with a ratio of 1.91:1, both landscape and horizontal. The minimum size of the image you can upload on Instagram is 600 x 315 pixels. But if you want to ensure good quality of the picture you are going to upload, then make sure the size of your picture you are uploading is at least 1080 x 1080 pixels or 1080 x ratio you prefer.

It's important that you make sure that the picture is taken in a good environment – clear and well-lit. It's also a good thing to be picky with the background you choose. It's best to pick a background that has a color that matches your feed or the color of your brand logo to make it more aesthetic and pleasing to the eyes.

But aside from being meticulous with the content to upload in your account, here are other important things you need to put your focus on when running your account:

5.2.1 Setting a Budget

Most of the time, the main concern of people marketing their products is as to whether or not they can afford the costs. Well, with good budgeting, you wouldn't spend more than you should or more than you could potentially earn from selling your products or services.

While advertising your products like posting photos, videos, or stories on Instagram is free, you can avail of the paid sponsorship by Instagram.

Choose a Budget

When running an Instagram ad, there are two budget options for you to choose from:

- Daily

- Lifetime

By setting your budget daily, the system will put a cap on how much you should spend on ads per day. On the other hand, the lifetime budget defines the max amount you are willing to spend on the entire duration of the campaign.

When deciding on how much budget you are going to put in place, choosing a schedule is also necessary. What time of the day do you want your ads to run and when do you want it to finish?

You have to manage your ad delivery as a part of determining your budget. You are able to go for link clicks, where Instagram uses the algorithm to get you the most engagement for as low money as possible.

Alternatively, you can work on your impression, where you can get your ads seen as many times as possible as long as it is within your budget. Or you could also go for day to day unique reach. This option is meant to display as many unique users as possible as long as it is within your budget.

Then, you have to decide whether you want to manually or automatically set your bidding amount. By choosing a manual, you are able to choose how much your maximum bid is. For automatic, on the other hand, you're letting the algorithm to decide for you. By setting your bid manually, you can outbid another competitor if you're willing to pay more than how much they bid.

It's best to use automatic bidding when you have a larger audience and you don't have a lot of competition.

On the other hand, if you have a small audience and intimidating competition, then manual bidding would be a better option. This can also prevent you from going beyond your budget.

Regardless of how much your bid is, it has to be based on the conversion value for your business. You must keep in mind that Instagram does not always know what this is — only you do. That being said, you must also keep in mind that not every audience will provide you with the same value. That's why you will want to modify your bids based on the audience you are trying to targeting.

Lastly, you have to choose whether or not you want to show your ads throughout the day (standard) or on a faster delivery pace (accelerated).

How Much are Instagram ads?

When you look further into the world of Instagram advertising, you will easily notice how the cost would make a huge impact on your decision as to whether you would do it or not. It's important to know how you could potentially spend as this allows you to maximize the result.

Compared to other social media platforms, Instagram is considered to be on the more expensive side. The reason for this is the fact that the way their advertising works consists of more work and brings in more conversions.

You can choose from these two cost models when getting ads from Instagram:

- Cost-per-impression (CPM)

- Cost-per-click (CPC)

For the CPM campaign, the average cost you would pay is $6.70 per 1,000 impressions. On the other hand, CPC campaigns would cost you between $0.20 to $2 per click. The total cost of your ads would highly depend on several factors.

Here four main factors that determine your Instagram advertising costs:

1. Bid Amount

The amount of your bid affects how much you spend on an ad campaign. You have to decide how much money you are ready to spend to attract new leads. This bid affects the money you spend as well.

Because Instagram has more expensive bid amounts. You'll want to be ready to pay more for each click and impression.

Okay, so if your budget for the campaign is $500 and your bid amount is $2 for each click, you are only able to get 250 clicks on the ad campaign you have. On the other hand, let's say you have a budget of $1000 with a $2 CPC, then you'll get 500 clicks. In this same case, having a bid amount of $0.50 will give you, even more, clicks with these two budget amounts.

The bid amount you put in will affect your budget and your budget will influence the amount of money you bid. These amounts are going to influence how much it costs you to put your ad on Instagram.

2. Ad Relevancy Score

Your ad relevancy score will also have an impact on your Instagram ads cost. Your relevancy score is how relevant Instagram considers your ad to be in relation to those who will see your ad.

Instagram wants to show relevant content to their audience in their feed. They will base your score on how people react towards your ad.

If people respond positively to your ad, your relevancy score will increase. It includes actions like clicking, commenting, liking, and more.

On the other hand, actions like hiding the ad cause a negative response. This will give you a lower ad relevancy score, which will hurt your ad's performance.

Ads with a high relevance score are placed over low relevance scores. Having a more relevant ad means you will pay closer to the minimum amount. You'll get more clicks on your campaign and drive more leads.

3. Estimated Action Rates

The estimated action rates have an effect on the prices of your Instagram advertising prices as well. According to Instagram, this rate is derived from the likelihood of people interacting with your ad. Basically, they want to know how much engagement you are likely to get with your ad.

These engagements involve actions like converting and clicking. Instagram chooses to promote ads they think will attract people to make engagement. If Instagram thinks that your ad is good enough to attract more people to make engagement, then, of course, they will place your ads first. This means you will get a lower bid amount. This will make you earn more conversions and leads.

4. Competition

The competition is always going to affect how much money you'll have to pay for your ad. If you are trying to target a certain demographic, then expect to face competitions trying to target the same audience. The number of competitions can also affect the amount you'll have to pay for the ads.

If it happens that there are other people trying to bid on reaching out to the same audience, then prepare yourself for a bidding war. Companies fighting over the audience might have to outbid each other to get to the top place.

Additional Factors

Here are additional factors that might affect the amount of money you'll have to pay to successfully advertise on Instagram.

- **Holidays and events**: For some reason, competition is higher throughout holidays, particularly Christmas. More companies are trying to compete to reach valuable leads, which of course, boosts up the CPC. You will have to consider these special holidays that surround the when running your ad as it will really impact your budgeting decision.

- **Gender:** Advertising to females is more expensive than advertising for males. This is because females are likely to make engagement with your posts compared to males, so basically, Instagram took advantage of this fact.

- **Day of the week**: It shows that Instagram users are more active, engagement-wise, during weekends, so this means that if you want to save on your budget, then you may want to put your ads up on weekdays.

- **Your market:** The market you are in also heavily influences the price you have to pay on your Instagram ads. It's more expensive for B2B companies to run ads since there are fewer businesses on the platform compared to people. Industries like apparel cost more because of high competition.

5.2.2 How Do Instagram Ads Work?

Instagram ads are paid content that shows up in the newsfeeds and stories of Instagram users even if they don't follow you. Instagram ads are shown to the users that Instagram thinks would be interested in your content or products the most.

People are shown Instagram ads derived from their demographic information as well as previous search history. These ads blend perfectly with normal ads posted by people the users follow so at first glance, you would not even notice that it was meant to be an ad and you're not even following the account that posted that.

But if you look clearly, there are some indications that tell whether a post is a sponsor or not. First of all, it's going to have the word "Sponsored" written below the username. Secondly, it's likely to have a call-to-action that shows under the picture – this usually directs you to a website.

Advanced Ad Budget & Schedule Options

Instagram offers some additional advanced options that will help you make your ad optimization better. In the platform, you are able to optimize the delivery style if ever you wanted to display an ad once a day or even multiple times.

Keep in mind that you want to make sure that you finish your placements and pick Instagram before editing these options on Post Engagement, Impressions or Daily Unique Reach. You must remember that regardless of what you choose here, you will be charged for when that engagement metric takes place.

That means by choosing Impressions, you are going to be charged for the cost of Impressions. However, if you choose Post Engagement, you are able to choose being charged for impressions or post engagements such as comments and likes.

Furthermore, you can decide when you want your ads to be posted or if you want it to run continuously. This depends on your preference. It's recommended to follow the standard option because it follows the user's pace and schedule for publishing the ads.

Instagram Ads budget

Through your Facebook account, you can set your budget to either daily or throughout the whole campaign. When you choose to set a daily budget, you can choose the maximum amount you're willing to spend. When your limit has been reached, the ads will stop working until the next day. The minimum budgets you set for your Instagram ads will be considered as a daily amount and apply no matter which budget option you pick.

If you choose to be charged per engagement, your daily minimum has to be at least $2.50. Low-frequency events like offer claims or app installs, have to be charged at a daily minimum of $20.

You have to decide on how much you want to spend on the entire campaign duration so Facebook can calculate how much Facebook is going to charge you on a daily basis. No matter how good or bad your ad performs, you'll be able to determine how frequently your ads will cost.

Now that you know how much it would cost you to run an ad on Instagram, deciding as to whether you're still going to do it or not should be easy. Now, let's move on to the more important step, which is creating your Instagram.

5.3 Creating your Instagram Ads

all bodies and races, then it's a good idea to put them on a model of different sizes and colors so that the followers get a vision on how the clothes would look on them if they decide to buy them.

Start with a goal

When creating a campaign, you have to start with the most important thing, which is coming up with your goals. This is a must for any and every campaign. So, what's your goal? If you're not sure, don't worry because Instagram can provide you with some options.

• • **Awareness**

What is your brand all about and what does it have to offer that people shouldn't refuse? You can use your Instagram account to answer these important questions. Use attractive graphics and colors to gain users' attention. Make sure to highlight the features of the products or services you are trying to offer.

For example, if you are trying to sell clothes that celebrate

• **Find potential customers**

Perhaps you're interested in more than just awareness. Perhaps, what you want is actual actions from the people you are trying to target. If that's the case, then you may want to have a contest that encourages you to follow you in order for them to have a chance to win. You can also encourage the people who will see the ads to sign up for your newsletter so they can get more updates about your brand in the future.

• **Drive more sales**

The most effective way to make sales through your ads is to create eye-catching images or videos giving away promo codes or coupons. You can also explain the advantages they can get from downloading your apps. If you have brick and mortar stores and you want people to come and visit those locations, then give them reasons to and show those reasons through your posts.

After deciding what your goals are, the next steps you need to do are to...

- **Identify your audience**

To make it easier for you to refine your target audience when creating

Instagram ads – create a buyer persona. It's normal for those who are new to the Instagram game to not know which audience they should be targeting – there's nothing wrong with that. After all, you will be able to know about it over time. However, if this is the case, you should go easy on spending money on ads, otherwise, you are likely to waste that money.

You want to be smart and plan your campaign and learn to reach people. It's pretty useless to reach out to 10,000 people a day that have zero interest in the thing you are trying to sell. Reaching out to 10 people who actually need the product you are selling will give you more potential for selling.

What you need to do is to plan your ad campaign by putting your audience as your priority. Okay, let's say your target audience is 25 to 39-year-old women located in the USA, then you have to take a little step further by using targeting options offered by Instagram and set your target setting for that specific group of an audience – you also have the option of using third-party tools.

You may also want to check out the engagement rates on your previous posts. This way, you will learn more about how your audience responds to your posts. This will help you prevent yourself from posting ads that are not doing well.

Figure out who your audience is if you've been on Instagram for a while, this should be an easier task. Based on the users who have been interacting with your posts, you can create a Custom Audience. You can use features by Ads Manager such as Custom Audiences that will allow you to retarget who have checked out your page and followed through your CTA, etc. You can also generate Custom Audiences by uploading business contact lists.

Fortunately, Instagram conveniently has to target features that offer different options in terms of picking the audience that will see your ads based on demographics. These demographics include gender, location, relationship, age, interests, etc.

This is how building your Core Audience works. However, you also have the option to go deeper and work around Behavioral Targeting. For example, do you want to target an audience that is married? Or maybe the ones who are working on a specific field? There are always options for that! Instagram advertising offers a wide variety of targeting options, but of course, the more specific you want your audience to be, the more complicated the process would be.

In order for you to measure your chart accurately, make sure to also check out Audience Size. With this chart, you will learn how narrow or broad your reach is. You have to make sure that your audience is not too wide and also not too specific. At the same time, you should not limit the prospective views you get. The right balance is the key, and this is something you need to master.

After creating a target audience for your Instagram ad, don't forget to save it in order for you to see it again when you need to.

Be open to testing different audiences in order for you to see what works best. You can do this by creating multiple ad sets, which is located at the top of the Instagram Ads Manager page.

Refine your content and message

There are brands that use sharp, visually focused content on their Instagram. This is common for travel-focused brands to help them portray that their goal is something to do with seeking adventure. The main aspect of your ad content is the message your brand is trying to deliver. By making your message as obvious as possible, visually-wise, it is going to resonate with your audience better.

Consider your voice: Should you make it formal or just casual? Deciding on your tone it is also important. Do you think it's better to sound more friendly and warm or are you aiming to sound more of in-your-face and intimidating?

Based on statistics, consistency plays a huge part here, with 60% of top brands making use of the same filter for every post they make. Keeping a consistent message will help you reinforce your brand in people's minds and at the same time, following with their core values.

An important part of the message you want to delivery is the angle you want to follow. Get to know your audience as this is going to be very helpful in choosing a strong angle. Learn what your customers truly want.

Once you figured out what your customers really want, hitting them with the angle would be the next step. For example, you can focus on giving them inspiration or motivation, which may blend with the virtue your brands want to showcase – this is what most sports brands do. Or you could simply focus on selling your products.

You can also consider using your ads to promote a cause or charity you are supporting. Today, more audiences like brands that support causes that matter to them. This means that partnering up with charity may help you get a new audience that shows support to those specific organizations.

Good content is something that can connect with your audience. If you want to learn more about what content is performing the best with your audience, use your analytics.

Create a unique hashtag

This is where you truly have to be creative. To make your campaign mark in people's minds, one of the best things to do is to create a hashtag specific for your brand. Hashtags are a wonderful thing for businesses. Their main purpose is to improve content discovery, but they can also create a community and a trend within your campaign, which is likely to generate more audience and engagement. It's actually very easy to create your own hashtag. The more challenging part is to make people use that hashtag, especially if you are not a big brand yet.

When making a hashtag, make it short and sweet – usually, three or four words is the maximum. Some of the good hashtags used by popular brands are:

- #LikeAGirl – Always
- #ShareACoke – Coca-Cola
- #IceBucketChallenge – ALS Association
- #PetsAtWork – Purina
- #LetsDoLunch – Domino's

These hashtags were some of the most successful ones created and as you can see, they clearly show what they represent and they are unique. You don't want to use a hashtag that someone has used before.

A good hashtag is short, easy to remember, and relevant to your brand or campaign. Those hashtags are meant to be included in your post and when people were interacting with your hashtag, make sure to interact with them back by liking their post or reposting their stories. This can encourage more people to interact with the hashtag.

Choose a placement

When you have got your content sorted out and you've successfully defined your audience and message together with your hashtag, fine-tuning your details would be the next step.

You will actually have 15 different placement selections you can choose from the Ads Manager. However, if you want to run Stories ads as well, then you must uncheck them all aside from Instagram Feed.

Choose a format

How do you want to show your ads as? Here are the options you have:

- Single image
- Video
- Stories
- Carousel
- IGTV

You must choose the format for your content based on your assets as well as marketing goals. After choosing the format for your ads, then you're ready to upload. You can also add a caption for the content, which is limited to 2,200 characters.

Add your website URL

It's very important to add your site URL, especially if your main goal is to drive traffic to your website or sell a product. If there are specific products you want to sell, then direct the URL to that specific link.

If you happen to be using marketing automation software, you will have to put together a unique tracking URL using UTM parameters. Otherwise, you will not be able to track the conversions and traffic you are trying to generate from your ad.

Make a headline

This is not necessary all the time since your audience cannot always see the headline of your ad. But then again, creating a short headline, just in case, wouldn't cost you extra. It has to be brief and has to describe where your potential audience is going to be directed to.

Add a call-to-action

Instagram ads did not perform well as expected when they were first launched. So, they knew they had to do something, and their idea was to add a CTA button to the ads – and it worked!

You can't add clickable links on the captions, and people love convenience. Many wouldn't be willing to take their time to go to their phone browser and type in a link written on the ads. But with CTA, they can simply click on the link and they will be directed where the brand wants them to go.

And it's not only convenient for the audience, but also for the brand's ad manager! They made setting up CTA easier. For example, instead of you requiring you to make a CTA entirely from scratch, you are able to choose from different options already available. These options are Sign Up, Watch More, Contact Us, Learn More, Donate, and Apply Now.

You can choose which CTA to add to your campaign based on your objective. The CTA is an extremely important part of creating ads, so you must learn how to make use of it the best way possible.

Run a final check before placing the order

If you are the only one to have seen the ads at this point, then you might want to show the ad to some member of your team before putting it out there.

If you're not ready to put your ads live just yet, you can set to publish it at a certain time of the day or even at later date. Once you're ready, just click on the place order button.

Track the performance

When your ad is live, you may want to keep track of its performance. You can make some modifications if you notice that it's not performing as expected.

The Facebook Ads Manager provides you with a thorough overview of your Instagram ad campaign. There is information on total ad spend, post shares, cost per result, app installs, video views, social clicks, total reach, and a lot more. It's a good way to test the water if you are new to this game.

This short step-by-step guide would be useful for any marketers who are trying to learn more about creating Instagram ads that really offer results. Come back to it whenever you create a new campaign and tick off every task mentioned. By doing all the steps mentioned, it's unlikely for your ads to not reach the right people at the right time and the right place.

Chapter 6: Instagram Monetization

It's easy to fall for the saying, "there's strength in numbers" and while it's true in many instances, this is not the case on Instagram. It doesn't mean that the more followers you have, the better.

For a time, there has been a trend where businesses and influencers buy bot followers. And while it truly increased the number of their followers, there have been no interactions and engagement from these ghost followers. And to make it worse, these inorganic followers unfollowed these accounts eventually. So, in the end, buying followers is just a waste of money.

We can't stress this enough, but the most important thing in social media campaign is the engagement. Followers that comment, like, tag their friends, and share your post are the strength of social media marketing. As long as you have these engagements, it doesn't matter whether you have 100 followers or 10,000 followers.

In this chapter, we'll talk about how you can use these numbers and engagements and turn them into earnings.

6.1 Effective Ways to Monetize Your Instagram Account

Okay, let's say now you have an active community that endlessly leave comments and likes on your posts and seem to be on the lookout on your next updates, how can you make the most of this?

Well, this all depends on your objectives.

Perhaps you're planning to have a partnership with brands as an influencer, or maybe working alone is something you like to do better. If you can't decide yet, don't worry, we have some recommendations.

- **Accepting Sponsored Posts**

Sponsored posts are becoming more and more popular among influencers today. The way it works is the same as uploading a regular content that you would usually upload to promote your brand, the only difference is that you are not uploading your own content, instead, you have to promote someone else's content in your own account and of course, you are going to be paid for doing it.

There are many reasons to love this kind of marketing but of course, you have to be very careful when doing this.

First of all, accepting sponsorship means you might be offered to promote something you are not well-familiar with. And as a brand that values people's opinion, you have to make sure that the brand or product you are promoting is not going to dent your image. For example, if you are a brand that is promoting campaigns against animal cruelty, and you are offered to promote beauty products, make sure that those beauty products are not tested on animals. People will always know and you might receive a lot of criticism for it.

Furthermore, if you are offered to do honest paid reviews on a product, don't be afraid to describe the product's shortcomings. And if that's something you do and stand for, make sure to tell the company who is sponsoring you that you might point out negative things about the products if necessary.

While it might sound counterintuitive at first glance, the genuineness of this form of promotion will take you a long way, and you'd be admired and preferred by brands and companies who are confident about their products trying to promote.

In order for you to find brands that are also looking for collaboration, you can use platforms that will help you like Tribe and Influence.co. Through these platforms, you can find partners that are more than willing to be promoted by you.

- **Contacting Your Potential Sponsor**

The aforementioned platforms will help you get the contact information of your potential sponsor. Now the next steps are on you. The way you approach the next step can make or break the deal. Here's how you do it...

Creating Your Pitch

When you successfully got the email address of the brands you need to contact, it's time for you to send in your pitch. Of course, you can't simply send out an email with your pitch and call it a day. You have to learn how to make the perfect pitch. Here are the important points you need to include:

Your Strengths

Sending a pitch is like promoting your products – you need to sell yourself. You need to point out the benefits the potential sponsor will get if they choose to have a partnership with you. You need to highlight your strengths along with the coverage of your influence.

Point out what you can bring on to the table and how you can make a difference. How much influence do you have within your community? What do you do to change people's lives for the better? Do you have any credentials to support or prove your expertise? What is your biggest achievement so far? These are some of the important things you can include in your pitch.

It's important to make sure that you're going to stand out – keep in mind that you have a great competition and your goal should be noticed. That's why selling yourself is the key to winning new sponsorships. But then again, you must also be picky about who you send your pitch to – do research to make sure that they meet your virtue and that their pay meets your standards.

What You Are Proposing, Exactly

Of course, you must include what you are proposing in your email. You don't have to be super detailed with this information at this point. You can give them a general idea first and when they respond asking for further details, that's when you can provide them with it.

For example, you don't have to tell them in detail how you are planning to create the content. You don't have to give them the concept just yet. This is something you can discuss and brainstorm later on throughout the negotiation.

Usually, a brand will show interest by asking you for your proposal – this is where you can impress them more.

Providing Call to Action

In your introductory email, it's important to include your general proposal, but you must also include a specific call to action. A form of a call to action is to recommend for them to request for your media kit as well as a list of performance so that they can review it.

The reason why you don't include these important elements in your initial pitch is that they are likely not a response to you back. Give them something to be curious about. The time while they are waiting for your response to their CTA, you're preventing them from doing rush decisions as to whether to hire you or not.

Your Pricing

You can give away your pricing on your first message, however, some don't include it until they are requested for media kit and proposal. And the reason for this is that some influencers would set their prices differently based on the type of content they are going to create as well as what brand they are pitching for.

If you are simply taking a picture of a product with a simple caption, then that has to be cheaper than having to make an entire video for the sponsorship. You surely have to spend more hours creating a video than just shooting and editing a single picture, so it just makes sense that the pricing is not fixed.

6.1.1 Sell Your Own Products

Today, most influencers sell something to their avid followers. This is not surprising especially that we're now we are living in an era where more merchant transactions are done online. And if you are someone with a big following, you will surely have great success in this. Seriously, just think of some of the online celebrities right now, can you think of someone who's not selling anything? Their merch might come in the form of clothing, music, makeup, recipes, workout plans, etc.

On the other hand, if you already have a brick and mortar store and created an Instagram to raise awareness, then you must consider expanding your transactions online. Again, people just love convenience! They would rather pay virtually and wait for their goodies to come in their doorstep than having to drive far for the product they need or want.

Selling your own products is just one of the best ways of monetizing through Instagram.

Perhaps you like painting – you can use your talent to sell some goods. Are you a videographer? Why don't you sell tutorials on how you make videos? Selling courses through Instagram is becoming more and more popular nowadays, so if you have specific skills you know you can share, don't be afraid to try this out.

Other physical merchandise you can sell to your followers include shirts, kitchenware, snacks, and just anything that is relevant to your niche.

There are tons of businesses from different fields that have succeeded in making sales transactions on the platform. These include online-based businesses, brick-and-mortar stores, and service-driven companies.

Selling Products Through DM

Another way of selling your product to people is through Direct Message or DM. But how does this work and how do you get to find these people who you can send these products to?

You can do this by writing a CTA in the caption that will help you notify who is interested with your products. You can write something like, "Comment YES if you want to learn more".

The great thing about sending a proposal through DM – although it can be time-consuming – is that you can build personal relationships with prospective clients. On top of that, you can send them clickable links! When sending them clickable links, however, it's best to shorten the URL as this will look more professional and also less annoying to the eyes of people who are meant to click on them.

Make Sure Your Site is Mobile-Friendly

Remember that Instagram is a mobile-based app and although it's already accessible on desktop, this version doesn't have DM and upload features. This means that if you want to make your audience more willing to go with your CTA, make it more convenient for them! You can do this by making sure that your website is 100% optimized for mobile browsers.

Other Important Tips to Know When Selling on Instagram

1. **Make sure you're running a business account.** Although you can always run a Personal account for your business, using Instagram Business accounts will provide you with more information about your brand and an analytics tool that will help you measure your success.

2. **Upload high-quality content.** Obviously, Instagram is highly

visual, so being able to present a professional-looking content is one of the main keys for boosting your engagement.

3. **Get your audience to relate.** There are three possible reasons why an Instagram user follows a business account. (1) They visually like the photos you upload; (2) they are interested in what you offer; (3) or they can relate to the stories being depicted by your content. Marketing through storytelling is an effective way to keep people engaged and make them talk about your brand.

4. **Use user-generated content.** Most of the shoppers always prefer making shopping-decisions based on their friends' recommendations, particularly on Instagram. So, if someone tags your account, whether on regular posts and stories, repost them on your account – this will encourage other users to trust your brand after other consumers trying and liking them.

5. **Make captivating Instagram ads.** You can also turn the user-generated posts into your own ads. This is better than typical photos that you would upload on your account.

6. **Partner with influencers and brand ambassadors to spread awareness.** Let people with big following do the marketing for you. People love them, and so the products they use! Partner with people with a strong influence on the platform and you will notice the flow of followers and new transactions coming in. These people have

the capability to promote your products and stretch your reach even further. As mentioned earlier, most consumers trust user-generated statements, and it's even better if it's from people they look up to.

7. **Speak to the customers.** Keep your current customers and gain the new one by featuring their photos on your profile or leaving comments in their posts. Building a relationship with your customers is an effective way to keep them coming back for more and gain new ones who want to be featured!

8. **Use hashtag discovery to find new followers.** On top of using paid advertisements, you can also take advantage of the hashtags to find new people to follow you and possibly to buy your products. Search for relevant hashtags and search for users who seem to be interested in the product you are trying to advertise. Follow them or leave a comment in their posts. This is a very effective way to find organic customers and followers.

9. **Make sure the profile link is always updated.** See to it that your profile link shows your current products or service that you are promoting.

10. **Offer promos and discounts.** As already mentioned in this book, everyone likes not paying for the full price. Giving them a time-limited discount will make them order products from you.

Sell More with Instagram Stories

Not only Instagram Stories are an amazing way to showcase what's happening within your business further than what you choose to show on your Instagram feed, but you can also use them to help you gain the interests of people who want to learn more about your products.

It would be beneficial to tease your products and promos through your Stories. Doing this prompts users to keep coming back to your page for more updates. Stories show up on top of the Feed, so they can easily get noticed. Stories would also be a perfect place for uploading content that you don't want to show up on your profile for more than 24 hours.

Instagram is also constantly testing new different features that can help brands to stand out more. One of the newer features of the platform is the Swipe Up feature, which unfortunately only available to users with at least 10,000 followers.

Instagram Testing Shopping Feature

Although there are a lot of tools that are able to help you grow income and boosts sales on the platform, the platform itself constantly keeps on improving its features to make it more beneficial for businesses. Not long ago, Instagram added the feature which allows brands to tag their products on the pictures they upload, and tag directs to the link where you can buy the product/s shown.

- **Sell affiliate products**

Affiliate marketing using your social media account builds a partnership between you and a company, where you will help them promote their products or services. This may work in two ways: First is via a pay-per-click basis where you are given a unique link to post on your page and every time someone clicks on it and buys products on the site through your link, you'll generate income. The other way is the company pays you a lump-sum for simply posting the link – it doesn't matter if someone clicks on the link or not.

The beauty of the affiliate marketing is that you don't have to have your own product to sell in order to generate an income – well, this applies for most forms of social media marketing. As stated earlier, this is a way to sell products without monetary investing in them and earning money on the process.

With that being said, it's extremely important to be knowledgeable about the products you are trying to sell. Make sure that it follows your personal principles. Before taking a plunge, it's important to educate yourself. When becoming an influencer, you have to be a role model for many, especially for younger audiences.

6.1.2 Affiliate Marketing
Here are some of the things involved in the process of promoting affiliate products on social media. Although it might sound simple, there are some important things you need to keep in mind to be able to be successful in it.

- **Creating Affiliate Redirect Links**

Internet users today are smart – they can easily recognize whether or not you are lying about a product you are selling. That's why you have to be creative on how you are going to integrate your affiliate links. You may want to make it simple and natural. Don't be too repetitive or pushy because this might put you off.

- **Prioritize Creating Quality Content**

When you are using social media to promote affiliate products or services, it has to be your main priority to create high-quality content. After all, creating quality content is your way to gain followers that will build your reputation online. You have to prove to your viewers all the time that you are a reliable source of information.

An engaging content that talks about news and current events and the latest trends where the product fits are another effective way to make this campaign effective. Your audience who are seeking this type of news is more likely to check out your link and may even end up buying your products or services.

Delivering high-quality content and promoting it within the content without being pushy will give you will generate amazing results.

- **Link Product Images**

A picture is worth a thousand words, and this is also the case when you are promoting something online. Adding high-quality, relevant pictures within your content is one of the most effective ways to grab people's attention.

After all, who wants to buy something without even seeing it? Making the most of the product images that will fit your social media for affiliate marketing posts will capture people's attention naturally. Taking pictures plays a huge part of being a content creator.

- **Shorten Your Links for Affiliate Redirect**

Putting long affiliate links on your content may appear unappealing. That's why it's important to make the link simpler by shortening it. You can use URLs using link management platforms like bit.ly, su.pr, and lnk.co.

- **Only Promote the Affiliate Products with Good Reputation**

No matter how good the quality of the product you are promoting is, how professionally put up together the link is, or how appealing the pictures are, if the product you are promoting is low quality, there will be a great chance that it's not going to work. Your social media for affiliate marketing is not going to be effective.

You have to keep in mind that when it comes to using your social media for money, your audience is your boss – you need to impress them and keep their loyalty.

By impressing your audience or followers with the kind of products you are presenting them, there is a better chance for them to engage in word of mouth. If they proved to themselves that you are being honest with your products, they can make the marketing themselves on your behalf.

- **Take Advantage of the Promotions**

Do you know what consumers love? Discount! So, if this is something you could do, offer to your followers, then your campaign is likely to be more effective! When asked for a partnership, ask the brand if they are able to provide you a unique affiliate code that your followers can use at check out and will give them a discount. This is a win/win situation for everyone! You win for getting a customer, the customer wins for getting a discount and the company wins for making a transaction!

- **Promote in Niche-specific Groups**

After creating your content, the next thing you may want to do, especially that you're just starting out, is to share your content with some of the forums or groups online. Facebook and LinkedIn make good platforms for sharing your content to promote affiliate products. Search for other groups that are relevant to the niche that the product lands at. Through this group, is where you can find the best prospective clients.

Furthermore, you will be able to find several communities online that promote different products that pay a high amount for affiliate partnerships. This will be a great gateway for you to find more resources. This kind of community is a great source for networks that will be very beneficial for your future projects.

Be the Influencer of Your Community

Having a social media community marketing is becoming more and more popular due to its effective and fast results. But the important question is that, what is this community? To put it simply, this is the community that you create within your target market. Some examples are the gaming community, makeup community, and fitness community.

It's important that you build a profile and reputation in order to build influence within this community. And this is, no doubt, the most important part of this whole process. Especially that people like ranking influencers based on their contribution within the community.

Keep in mind that the success of your campaign is mainly based on the reputation and credibility of you along with the product you are marketing. So, before the money you will get from marketing a certain product, ask yourself first – is this something that will boost my credibility or at least not ruin it?

6.1.3 Selling Products for Commissions

One of the popular ways of earning money today through Instagram is with affiliate marketing. As Instagram continuously becoming popular all over the world and more and more people use it as a way of entertainment, self-expression, and communication, business giants and startups alike take advantage of it to promote their businesses.

If you are an influencer looking to use your account for affiliate marketing, your goal is to attract as much traffic as possible through your affiliate links. With Instagram boasting engagement better than other social media platforms like Twitter and Snapchat, affiliate marketing through Instagram offers a great opportunity for people looking to earn money and at the same time, offers a way for brands to get more sales.

Now, we are looking at Instagram affiliate marketing from the perspective of both influencer and the brand because as an Instagram user, you could either one of them or both.

How Does Instagram Affiliate Marketing Work?

Instagram affiliate marketing is done by building a partnership between a user (affiliate marketer) and the owner of the products (usually a company or a brand). Basically, the owner of the products being marketed asked the Instagram user to promote their products and provide a unique link that directs to either their homepage site or to a specific product that could be added to the cart. Once people start clicking on links and buying products on the site through the unique link, the Instagram user gets his or her commission.

The affiliate marketer describes the product or service within their postings and gets a commission on every sale that's made that could be attributed to their post, like through a URL link that has been used to redirect the customer to the site or with the use of unique discount code.

The brand that is being promoted and advertised gets inherent customer interest and the influencer that is working as the affiliate is used to convince its followers towards the product being marketed. The influencer gets some when a sale is made because of them. So, this form of campaign is obviously beneficial for parties. No wonder why more and more influencers swear by it.

Where does the influencer put the link if Instagram doesn't allow clickable links in the posts?

As you know already, Instagram is not link-friendly unlike Facebook, Twitter, and other social media sites. So, if this is the case, how can it be affiliate marketing-friendly? Here is how this works.

Adding Affiliate Link in Your Bio

- **Permanent**

As mentioned earlier, even though you cannot leave clickable links on specific posts, this is something you can do in the bio. So, if you see someone promoting something, instead of leaving a link, they'd probably just write something along the line, "link in the bio". You can leave a link in the bio for as long as the campaign goes. This is how you'd want to do it if you are constantly promoting the same brand that requires you to direct to the same link. This is ideal for brand ambassadors and exclusive affiliate endorsers.

- **Semi-Permanent**

On the other hand, if you are planning to post different products, then you might have to update the link in your bio constantly. However, when changing the link in your bio, you must also update the caption in your posts because when someone stumbles upon your old post, they might check your bio and end up being directed to a different link. So, this might require more work, but then again, more efficient as you don't want to just promote a single product the whole time.

Instagram Story

As mentioned earlier, a newly added feature that is only available for business accounts with at least 10,000 followers is the Swipe Up on Stories. This is a feature that allows the business owners to add a link in their Story accessible by swiping up. But of course, this will only appear on the site for 24 hours, just like any other Story. This is a more convenient way to share an affiliate link because you don't have to update your bio every so often.

Unique Discount Code

Instead of a unique affiliate link, some companies would rather provide their influencers with a unique discount code. This is easier because they don't have to worry about Instagram not letting them put clickable links on their caption. The Instagram user can simply write the code in capital letters within the caption or put it in the picture to be uploaded. This is also ideal for people who don't have the Swipe Up feature yet as they can use their Story for their affiliate campaign.

Why Do Companies Need Affiliate Partnerships?

Affiliate partnerships, when done right, is highly beneficial for both parties and also the consumers. But let's get down to all the main reasons why companies need affiliate marketing more than anyone else.

- **Higher brand awareness, following, and engagement**

Once a picture of a product or service is posted on the platform, the influencer usually tags the Instagram account of the company or brand who created it. When people saw that, they are likely to check out the account that is tagged and follow them to see more of the product and possibly inquire to them about the product. This is a big plus for both influencer and company as it boosts the traffic and it brings in potential transactions. And more importantly, it raises brand awareness.

- **New relationships**

From the perspective of the brand, this form of marketing can generate new relationships with the influencers that help them generate more sales and following.

When an influencer successfully generated sales, it gives him or her the opportunity to continue doing the business with the company – it's not going to be just a one-time deal. Similarly, if the influencer thinks that his or her followers like what they are endorsing, then he or she would be more than willing to continue promoting the products. These corporate relationships can greatly benefit both parties as both of them are eager to please and benefit each other.

- **Higher revenue**

With more than 1 billion users and 1 million active monthly users, not trying out Instagram affiliate marketing as a brand is one of the biggest mistakes you might do. These days, Instagram has seen a huge increase in PR and marketing channels over the platform whose main purpose is to advertise products and brands. With this, both brand and Instagram itself see higher revenue and engagement with Instagram affiliate links.

Aside from people they know in person, a typical Instagram user follows a celebrity, and these people look up to these people. So, many of these people tend to have the same thing in common with these celebrities/influencers – from the clothes they wear to the food they eat and exercise they do, many people imitate them, so when these influential people endorse something, many people are going to be hypnotized and follow their call-to-action.

Can Anyone Be Successful at This?

Unfortunately, not everyone who has an Instagram account can easily be successful and qualified for affiliate marketing. There are certain qualities and requirements set by companies before they decide to close a deal with you. Here are those

- **Someone Who Values Their Community**

A good Instagram affiliate marketing partner is someone who doesn't only give value to their brand but also its community. A good influencer should be able to hold a positive influence on people who look up to the brand. As much as possible, brands avoid influencers who are controversial. They tend to avoid those who have a negative buzz around their name. Similarly, the brand must have a competitive influence within the niche or market the brand belongs to.

- **Someone Who Has a Good Number of Following**

This is one of the main requirements of the brand – they want the influencer to have a lot of followers. There is no specific for what considered a good number, but usually, it should be at least 5,000 or engagement-wise, something that makes at least 100 likes per posts. This is to make sure that the followers are not bots or paid followers. At the end of the day, engagement is more important than the number of followers. So, whether you are a nano-influencer or a micro-influencer, the more important thing is that you have a good flow of engagement.

- **Someone Who Has Relevancy**

It's pretty unlikely for a reputable fashion influencer to promote something related to technology. It just doesn't look good for both influencer and the company as it seems like they are shoving something to someone's throat that even the influencer is not actually interested in based on the niche he or she is running.

That's why most companies have to evaluate the influencer's posts as to whether or not they have an audience with the same interests and that they will actually enjoy it.

This involves deep searching and the company might even have to go through each post to confirm the relevancy of their products or brand with the influencer's account.

Similarly, for the influencers, they must be picky when it comes to choosing which products or brands, they should represent in order to assure the relevancy.

Transitioning from a Personal Instagram Account to Affiliate Marketer

So, if at this point you've already made up your mind that you want to try out affiliate marketing, there are some important things you must consider before starting an affiliate marketing relationship. Here are some tips you need to do in order to be successful in this endeavor.

- **Increase your Instagram following**

While you don't necessarily need to have hundreds of thousands of followers, it would really be beneficial better to have organic followers who make regular engagement. The more engagement, the more chances for you to have a chance to be successful at this. There are many ways to learn how you can grow your following on Instagram, which we will discuss later in this book. It's actually not as difficult as it might look, it's the same as building other social media following for your personal account, and it just mainly involves socializing. Interacting and following people who are interested in your niche would be the easiest. If you are a beginner, you might want to dedicate some of your time leaving about 5 to 10 comments a day in order to improve your engagement.

- **Use hashtags wisely**

Hashtags are a wonderful thing for businessmen trying to promote their brand and items on social media as this is one of the most powerful tools to get discovered. It seems like everyone uses hashtags on everything, make sure to take advantage of this! This is not an overnight process, but by making use of the right hashtags, you can gradually build strong credibility overtime. You must always keep it relevant all the time, though!

- **Always take it easy**

Attracting the potential users of the product you are marketing is the main goal of Instagram affiliate marketing, and this process requires a lot of patience. Just take it easy because rushing things out wouldn't take you anywhere. Furthermore, you have to make sure that your posts are filled with good vibes and not only blatantly promoting products need to be sold.

In order for you to do this, you have to make sure that you are posting high-quality photos that are interesting or inspiring for your followers. It should not only be of a particular product but must rather have some interesting features to it. For example, if you are selling active clothing, you could upload a picture of a woman wearing your gear stretching with beautiful nature as the backdrop – this will give the person who sees it a sense of relaxation. It doesn't mean you have to own expensive cameras or you need to take photography classes to take the best picture, but put the effort into it to add some aesthetic to your post.

If you're fully convinced that Instagram affiliate marketing is something you know you can be successful at, then don't be afraid to try it out. Just make sure that you have a good portfolio that will make you stand out in the sea of influencers trying to make the name for themselves as well. This is why it's important for you to keep existing relationships strong and keep making new ones. Strategies about your goals have to be realistic expectations.

Affiliate marketing is not always seen positively in society, but when done right and done with the right people, this can definitely work wonder with all parties involved.

6.1.4 Selling your Pictures

Do you realize how much time people spend on Instagram creating the perfect post? No one can tell exactly, but one thing is for sure – it's a lot of time! From shooting the photos, picking the right one, and adding the right filter, it takes hours! With all that effort, you better get something valuable with that! And another thing you can do to earn money from your Instagram is selling the content in it!

And the best thing is that you can actually make a handsome amount of money out of your Instagram pictures, even outside the platform.

Sell Instagram photos online

Brands love authentic photos, but with today's world when everyone seems to be taking pictures every second of everything, it seems like extraordinarily unique photos are hard to come by. This is an amazing opportunity for Instagram users who have beautiful pictures they are ready to let go.

There are two effective ways to go with this:

1. Selling individual photo

2. Sell thematic photo packages

Both come with their own characteristics and can be used for different purposes. Normally, individual photos are the kind that is breathtaking, unique, and just intriguing.

On the other hand, thematic photos are the ones that are generically classifiable images. Some examples of these are sky, nature, houses, mountains, and the like.

So, how can you make this work?

The first step is to identify which photos you think are going to be interesting for brands and companies to buy. Similarly, choose which photos you think you can group together thematically, and which ones you want to sell as an individual.

And then choose places to sell those pictures on.

Here are some of the popular places to sell your beautiful Instagram images:

Candidly Images

Candidly Images is a stock photo site where you can get your authentic images sold. So, basically, it's a photo site for people looking for stock photos, but unlike typical stock photos, they are geared towards photos that are unique and more natural-looking rather than cheesy and generic.

The good thing about this is that anyone can easily sell their Instagram pictures in it. You don't have to be a professional photographer with a big portfolio to be accepted to sign in. Photos are usually sold for $10 each and 50% of the profits go to the seller. This is a good way to earn fast cash, especially that the site does an amazing job marketing the photos that are up for sale.

Twenty20

Another stock photo site you may want to check out is Twenty20. It also allows Instagram photo submissions which make it easy for the sellers to earn money. Photos that are being submitted can be licensed for both editorial and commercial purposes.

Don't forget to add tags in the photos' description with all the relevant keywords in order to help your potential buyers to find p the pictures you are trying to sell. Use the same hashtags you would use on Instagram when you are uploading something. For example, if you are uploading a picture of a man riding a boat, some of the tags you can use are a *man on a boat, fisherman, boat in a lake, man fishing, boat ride,* etc.

The problem, however, is that the compensation is lower at only about $2 per picture. But then again, remember that you can sell as many photos as you want and when added up together, you can still make quite good money.

Instaprints

Unlike the first two mentioned, this one allows you to set your own price for your pictures. Instaprints, as its name suggests, prints your pictures and sell it to those who like them. All you have to do is to take the pictures, upload them, set the price, and wait for it to be sold. Instaprints takes care of the printing

Your Instagram photos can be printed in different sizes and can be printed in canvas, mugs, shirts, phone cases, and other accessories. Sellers are paid every 15th day of the month via PayPal or in check.

Clashot

Clashot is another platform you can use to sell your Instagram photos online. Install their app on your mobile phone, upload photos, and they will be up for sale for as long as you want. As long as they are selling, you can earn residual income.

What makes this different from other sources in this list is that they have moderators that make the decision as to whether or not the photos you upload are qualified for selling. Once they passed the moderators, then they will be up for sale. In order to make sure your photos will pass their standards; you may want to check the photos that are already uploaded on the site. This way, you will have an idea of the quality and themes that are more in demand.

Your photos can be sold from $0.50 to $80. When you earned $50, that's when you are able to withdraw your money.

Foap

Foap is another popular outlet for buying and selling Instagram photos. It was reported that some of the giant companies like Sony also come here to buy photos for their ads and campaigns! It also has gotten some media exposures so you can assure that they can legitimately help you make some money.

Just like Candidly, you can sell your pictures here for $10 and you get to keep the 50% in the sale leaving you with $5 each sale.

When selling your Instagram photos on theses platforms, remember that because these are considered stock photos, you're not selling the exclusive rights to your photos, which means you can sell them over and over again to different buyers.

Selling the Rights

Oh, you like the idea of selling the exclusive rights to the photos you've taken? There's a way for that too! Selling your Instagram photos can make you a lot more money and also faster.

You can approach brands and offer them your pictures. Now, in this case, they might not want to buy photos that were already uploaded on your Instagram, so how does this work? Well, you will just have to use your Instagram as your portfolio.

You can also have the photo you want to sell them prepared. You can send them the photos you want to sell watermarked but also show your Instagram account for further reference.

6.2 General Tips for Selling Products and Services Solely on Instagram

No one can deny that Instagram has become an amazing tool for many businesses. Unfortunately, this always doesn't work for everyone. There are key pieces businesses need to have in order to boost their potential in the sea of competition. Those keys are the following:

1. High-quality pictures of the products

2. Accurate measurement

3. Contact information

4. Payment and shipping method

5. Regions covered by shipping

Fortunately, these details are something you can easily incorporate in your profile – they may come in the form of bio descriptions, photos, or stories. Aside from uploading the pictures of the products, your Instagram profile is also a good place to tell your clients about your method of payment, shipping details, return policy, as well as how they can reach you outside the platform. When selling products, don't forget to include accurate measurements or dimensions.

Explain to people how they can place an order. Make sure to tell them to contact you via DM or leave your email address so that you can place an order. After you give a confirmation that the products of interest are available, then you can ask for shipping information and method of payment.

Sounds simple, right? The truth is, the way it works is not complicated, the more challenging part is how you can make people start buying from you. Once you get your first few transactions, it shouldn't be too hard after that.

With 1 billion users and about 300 million users visit at least one business profile a day, more than half of them do it to find new products to buy. No wonder why Instagram is becoming more and more popular among businessmen.

Now, if you are a small startup brand who doesn't have a website and want to set up a business by doing it on Instagram, here are important things you need to consider:

1. Choose Products that Sell

Because Instagram is a visual-focused social platform, selling products with a strong visual identity it makes things more effective. Here are some of the most popular products being sold on Instagram:

- Apparel
- Accessories
- Beauty products
- Home goods & decor
- Food & beverages
- Outdoor & fitness goods
- Auto parts

When it comes to digital product ideas, here are some popular ones:

- Graphic design
- Coaching services
- Food recipes
- Presets
- Online courses

If you already have products in mind, that's great! If it's not listed above, no problem. No matter what line of business you are trying to run, as long as you put yourself into it and you have strong passion and dedication for it, it's likely to succeed. When it comes to running a business on Instagram, coming up with a captivating story and engaging content it the most important thing to make people follow you and purchase your product.

2. Switch up to Business Profile

The importance of using a Business Account has already been mentioned earlier, but it deserves to be pointed out more than once. An Instagram business profile is like an interactive business card – except it offers a better marketing experience. Aside from being a great way to get prospective clients, it also serves as a channel for keeping connected with customers. Unlike the Personal Instagram profile, Business profile offers a lot of practical features, like the following:

- Being able to add important business information to your profile
- Statistics/Insights that help you learn about how your posts perform
- Post promotions that help you drive business objectives

3. Produce Engagement-Worthy Content

Creating quality content might be more of an indirect way of selling your goods. But the truth is that nothing can build a company's identity on Instagram better than quality content. No matter how new you are and how many competitions you have, as long as you can make your content stand out, you can always make your campaigns as effective as the biggest names in the industry.

4. Take Advantage of the Link You can Add in the Bio

So, here's the truth – the reason why Instagram doesn't allow its users to add a link in the posts is that they don't want the user to leave the app and switch to another platform. But at least they are considerate enough to allow one clickable link within your profile, and that's the URL you can leave in your bio.

But because you are an online social media-based online shop, you probably don't have your own website (yet) and that's okay! What you have for sure is a Facebook page – after all, you can't create a Business profile without a Facebook page. So, you may want to at least put it on your bio.

Every time a new customer sees your Instagram profile, they are likely to go to your bio page and see your link and likely to check it out. So, have it up there so you can have more followers on your Facebook page.

You can also just refer your new followers to the link up there. Make use of the "link in the bio" line to lead your followers to your page. This is a great CTA because it's actually very effective.

When the time comes you have to direct your followers to a new link, don't be afraid to change the URL with a new one.

You can also include a call-to-action in your bio. Anywhere within your bio, write something like SHOP NOW or DM US. This might sound like a simple action, but they actually do wonder as they usually work.

5. Add Links to Stories

Okay, again, this is only available to Business Pages with at least 10,000 followers (more reason why you should aim to grow your following) and once you reach this number, you have to make sure that you put this feature to good use. Not only this is an effective way to keep your followers stay engaged, but it's also an amazing way to generate sales.

Adding a URL to the Instagram Story is a big trend. It is highly beneficial to the brands or publishers who want to sell anything to generate transactions and drive more people to follow them.

In order to add links to your story, you just have to upload a photo in your Instagram Story section as you normally would. Tap on the chain icon located on the top right area and then enter the URL. Once you uploaded it, your followers will see a "See more" at the bottom which they can swipe up in order for them to be redirected to the link.

6. Use Instagram Advertising

One of the problems businessmen face when they are trying to advertise on Instagram is not being able to find the right people to advertise their products. This is where Instagram Advertisement comes handy. As explained earlier, buying Instagram sponsorship allows you to be shown in the feed of Instagram users who don't follow you but might be interested with your what you are trying to offer.

When running an ad on Instagram, you can decide on:

- How much you're willing to spend on the ad
- The demographic you want to cover
- How long you want the campaign to run for

You have total control of what your campaign is going to be about and that's one of the beauties of it. From the content to be shown to the audience who will see the ads, and to the total duration of the campaign – all these things are under your hands.

When it comes to the format, there are several options to choose from. Here are those options:

- Carousel ads
- Photo ads
- Slideshow ads
- Stories ads
- IGTV
- Video ads

You can easily make ads straight from your Instagram app. Just tap the "Promote" button located under the post or do it through the Facebook Ad Manager.

Make sure to do your research before you go ahead and create your ad. See your competitions and observe how they run their ads. This will help you make better decisions and make you stand out from the crowd.

7. Use the Shopping Features

The tagging feature of Instagram is a blessing to many businesses – not only makes it easier for followers to access the details and price of the products, but it also makes the page looks more professional-looking.

Although some of the big retailers were hesitant to use it when it was the first launch, which was kind of surprising, this feature definitely comes with a lot of benefits. Here are other reasons why using this feature can help your business account significantly:

- Within a single tap, customers are able to access more information about the products
- You are able to tag up to 5 products per photo or 20 products per carousel
- Customers are able to click "Shop now" and get directed to the site where they can place the order

Right now, this feature is only available in selected countries, and in order to set it up, there are the requirements you need to meet. You must...

- Integrate your Facebook channel into the store
- Have an approved Facebook store
- Have an e-store

It can be tricky to make shoppable Instagram posts because the feature is fairly new. But taking your time to learn how to get around with it would be worth it.

8. Use Instagram Selling Tools

So, what if the previously mentioned app is not available in your country? Or you're simply looking for more ways to make your Instagram business better and more effective? Well, you must consider using Instagram selling tools.

First of all, you have to know that Instagram selling tools are third party companies that offer software in order to make your feed shopping-friendly. These tools are able to help you monetize your channel in creative means – such as leaving comments or using hashtags. The only thing you have to do is follow your customers' preferences.

Here are some of the options you have:

- **Storefront link in the bio**

This is a great option if you are not using Shopping on the Instagram feature. This will allow you to build a shoppable storefront with the use of another app. So, what it does is it makes a link to a shoppable page that has a similar design as your feed on Instagram. But the thing is that this site allows the customers to tap the images to be redirected to the products the customer is interested in and that leads them to the e-commerce platform. Some of the apps you can use for this are Have2HaveIn and Like2Buy.

- **Selling via commenting**

Today, buying something can be as easy leaving a comment on a post, especially with the use of comment-buying tools. Two of the common tools for this are Soldsy and Spreesy. How it works is you have to install the app and then upload the product images through the app's dashboard. The apps then turn the images into shoppable posts. This allows the customers to buy the items directly by commenting "sold" along with other important information such as quantity, color, size, etc.

- **Selling via #hashtags**

There are also apps that allow you to sell using hashtags – you basically have to use the same bio-URL-to-storefront process. But with this, you are able to add a specific hashtag, which makes it easier for users to find the shoppable content. You can add the hashtag of the particular app to your description in order for potential buyers to notify you that the item is up for sale. Some of the apps that can be used for this are Boost or Inselly.

- **Selling via affiliate links**

Not only some apps are extremely useful in running a business on Instagram, but they also offer a great opportunity for building affiliate relationships with other companies. You can use apps like LikeToKnow.It, which embeds product credits using affiliate links. The moment someone "likes" the Instagram post, they're going to get an email that tells them more about the products. When someone purchases the products your posts feature, then you get a commission.

In order to make this more effective, you may want to let people aware that the products being shown are shoppable. You can't expect people to automatically know that they can buy the products you post. You can publish some photos, videos, or stories that will let your followers aware that they are able to shop on your profile. You can tell this via caption or on your bio.

9. Reach Out to Influencers

Today, Instagram collaborations have an excellent role in social media strategies. Consumers are getting smarter and smarter these days that they don't easily trust advertisements – instead, they would rather trust real people with real reviews. This is why influencer marketing has become the fastest-growing Instagram marketing method.

As already explained earlier in this book, a business teams up with an influencer in order to represent in selling their product. And basically, anyone with a big following and social media presence and engagement can be an influencer.

If you are still hesitant as to why you should try this method, here are the important reasons why you should:

- It's easier for you to target the right audience with the help of influencers. Because they already built their organic followers, you can assure that your message will be delivered to real people.
- It builds trust from the consumers. It's very important for a company to build a reputation to reach its sales goals.
- It can be cheaper compared to traditional advertisements.
- It bypasses ad blocks because posts from social media posts don't get blocked, you can assure that the ads will be seen.

So, here's how you'd do it...

1. Search for Instagram users that resonates with the kind of audience you are looking for. Search for someone in the same niche as yours who would be happy to try out your products. Always remember your campaign's goals and list the traits you need.
2. Create a schedule. How many posts do you want the influencers to post on your behalf? What kind of post? It's a good idea to plan your calendar accordingly in order to make it easier for the influencer to follow your schedule.
3. Make a deal. The biggest social media influencers like the Kardashians earn up to 250K for a just single post! But you don't have to pay that big right away. And actually, it doesn't have to be about financial compensation. You can make a deal with the influencers and tell them you're just starting up so all you can offer for now are free products.

Remember that size doesn't always matter. You don't have to stress about it if you can't afford to pay hundreds of thousands to pay an influencer. Working with multiple micro-influencers might be more effective than working with just one influencer with a larger following.

All in all, always keep in mind that the engagement Instagram can offer to your business is huge. And if you are not using it yet, then you are missing a lot. But at the same time, you shouldn't assume that you can only leave it all to Instagram – you can always go beyond the conventional way of marketing your business on the platform.

As much as possible, try cross-promoting on other social media platforms to make sales. Spread awareness on Facebook, Twitter, YouTube, and everywhere else. Let people know what's going on.

This is not only going to boost your sales but it will also build your image as a reliable and influential brand.

6.3 Instagram Marketing Dos and Don'ts

Now, let's just have a little refresher on what things to do and what to avoid in marketing through Instagram. Here are important things you must consider:

DO

- **Set up a good bio.** People are supposed to check out your Instagram profile all the time, so you better be able to let them know who you are and what you have to offer the first few seconds they are on your profile. Otherwise, they're just going to leave. Again, straight to the point bio is ideal. Make use of all the features and add all the important information – contact number, email address, website, etc. Make sure that it's going to be easier for them to contact you in case they need to buy something from you.

- **Post regularly.** It's important to post on a regular basis. Ideally, at least once a day. The audience and engagement can help you determine how often you should post and what time of the day.

- **Tag your locations.** If you have to attend an interesting event, having collaboration with known influencers or brands, tagging your resources would come in many advantages. There is a good possibility for your posts to get reshared and get a bigger audience.

- **Use filters right.** Make sure to put an effort making your content more visually appealing. While the most important thing in your business is to deliver the message, you're still on Instagram, which means, you're still on the platform meant to share beautiful photos and videos.

- **Be one of the tribes.** This is the most important thing when it comes to Instagram business. The key to building a relationship with your following is making engagement and interactions with them. To gain someone's loyalty, you want to make them feel like you acknowledge their presence. Like their comments, reply to them, follow them back – they will appreciate it and they will love you more.

- **Use hashtags.** Yes, using too many hashtags on a post might seem too spammy, but there's a way to get away with that. That is instead of writing the hashtags in the caption, just write it on the comments. Better if you wait for people to leave at least a couple of comments before you leave the hashtags, it's easier for the hashtags to get buried away if you do it like that.

- **Always think about what your goal is.** With most businesses, their main goal is to gain more followers or get new clients. Do all the things you can to reach those goals. You want them to check out your site? Let them know! Or maybe you want them to contact you... then make sure to provide them with your contact information! Learn how to use call-to-action properly and in no time, you will be able to learn how it works wonder.

DON'T

- **Only focus on high-quality photos.** Instead of aiming to just give them some *eyegasm*, you'd also want to give them something they can relate to. After all, that's more important. Furthermore, don't be afraid to show them some behind the scene of how your business run. Your followers will feel more connected to you when you show a personal business level with them.
- **Post too many times a day.** The ideal number is only 1 to 2 times a day. Posting too many contents a day may annoy your followers and they may lead for you get unfollowed.
- **Mix your personal profile and business profile together.** Yes, we mention to not be afraid to share who you are, but there should be a fine line between what you should share and what you should keep away from professional purposes. Your profile should be about your business – unless you run your account as an influencer, it will be quite inappropriate to share your selfies in it or other things that are not relevant to the product you are trying to sell.

- **Forget adding captions.** Your content wouldn't mean anything without the caption. Use your creativity and make captions that are captivating! Tell people about the photo and use this opportunity to add CTA.
- **Post content consecutively.** If you are planning to add multiple photos in the same day, you may want to space them out. If you are planning different photos of the same thing, you may even want to post them a day apart. You don't want to annoy your followers with the same content because they may unfollow you. Furthermore, because the Instagram algorithm is hard to read, it would be easier for more of your followers to see your posts about the same subject in case they missed it the first time you uploaded.
- **Upload photos that are a screenshot.** Do yourself a favor and don't upload anything that is a screenshot. Not only it will look unprofessional, but the quality is just pixilated and bad. Make an effort to only choose photos taken by you.
- **Overanalyze.** You don't have to spend hours contemplating what to upload or what to write as a caption. Just stop. Instead of spending too much of your time thinking too much, why don't you spend your energy engaging with your followers? The key is using creativity and being yourself.

Easy right? Earning money on Instagram by running a business on it shouldn't be too complicated, as you can see on the dos and don'ts mentioned above.

Chapter 7: Tips for Creating High-Quality Content for Your Instagram

7.1 How to Create the Perfect Pictures for Your Instagram Business Page

There are millions of pictures and videos being shared on Instagram every day. So, with this being said, how can you stand out and attract users to engage in your post?

The answer? Perfect content!

But in laymen's terms, what is perfect content? As a business, you need to portray your company as something organized, well-made, and well-thought-of. This can reflect on the pictures and videos you upload, so you have to make sure that your content has good composition, great colors, and tones, and is well-lit. Your choice of filter and effects play a huge part too!

Sounds like the job of a professional photographer or photo editing expert? Not really. By the end of this chapter, you're likely to be someone who can produce professional-looking content without having to go through photography class or spending hours trying to understand how photo and video editing works

7.1.1 Tips to Creating the Perfect Picture
1. Get Good Lighting

Making sure that you're getting good light is one of the key ingredients of creating the perfect photo for your Instagram business. No matter what kind of picture you are trying to capture, there's no amount of filter that can rescue a poor-lit picture.

As much as possible, use natural light as your source. So, if you are planning to take pictures outdoors, early morning or late afternoon photoshoots would be the ideal time. These times of the day are when you can get some of the beautiful outputs under natural lights.

2. Use Strong Colors and Shapes

Nothing can beat a photo with defined colors and shapes as these characteristics can truly make your photos stand out. It's best to choose and focus on an element that will appear large within your frame. By doing this, you will be able to draw your audiences' attention to your content.

Expressing emotion through your photos is also one of the best practices. If you're new to photography, capturing emotions through pictures may take time. But as you do it more often and you keep practicing, it will start coming naturally. Again, you don't have to be an expert to capture the perfect pictures. Just like any other skill, it's something that can be practiced and be good at overtime.

3. Learn How to Use Editing Apps

There was a time when Instagram users solely depended on the preset Instagram filters to use on their posts. Admittedly, it was cool at that time, but today, with the number of free editing apps that can help you create professional-looking edited pictures, there's no excuse to still use them.

Using these free editing apps, you can easily enhance that look and overall quality of your pictures. Gone are the days you need to learn how to be an expert on Adobe Photoshop to enhance your photos. Some of the user-friendly alternatives can be downloaded right straight to your smartphones. Some of these are VSCO, Snapseed, PicsArt, and RNI Films, but of course, don't be afraid to shop around for the best tools that meet your needs and requirements.

Another good thing about these apps is that they connect you with some of the professionals where you can get inspiration from. For example, VCSO is not only a photo editing app but also a photo-sharing community that aims to encourage people to show their creativity with the use of the apps.

4. Put Grids to Good Use

Many people look over the benefits offered by simple grids on their phones or cameras, but with the right usage, these grids can give you amazing output. For perfect Instagram shots, properly align all the elements of the pictures using these grids. Turning on the grid features can help you enhance the overall impacts of the picture.

It's important to observe carefully the overlapping elements on the screen in order to find the subjects' midpoint. As soon as you successfully get the center of the pictures, take the picture. Using the grid features can definitely make a huge difference no matter what kind of photography you are trying to achieve.

5. Use Your Eyes Before Your Lens

One of the biggest misconceptions in photography is that as long as you have high-end cameras, taking great pictures would be a piece of cake – this can't be any more wrong. The truth is, no matter how expensive your gears are, if you don't have good eyes for photography, your photos wouldn't be as great. Similarly, you don't have to own expensive cameras just to take high-quality photos.

To be able to get professional-looking pictures, it's important to train your eyes accordingly. Instead of taking thousands of pictures to get one perfect shot, take your time and learn how to get the best angles and compositions without the use of a lens. Before pressing the shutter, take pictures with your eyes first. By taking your time to observe what you may capture, you will have better ideas of how you can take the perfect pictures.

6. Use the "Less is More" Ideology

For beginners, one of the biggest mistakes they do when editing pictures for their business is over-editing them. And then most of the time, they just end up being so unappealing. To enhance your pictures, a little editing is enough. Keep in mind that you are editing photos to make your products look as it was taken by a professional photographer, you're not taking it to make it as if it was a part of a fiction movie. On top of it, if you are selling products, you don't want to make your products look different from what it looks like in real life or your customer will get disappointed.

What you want is to apply just some basic editing, which includes adjustments with the brightness, contrast, shadows, highlights, and temperature. What you have to be careful of is adjusting the saturation as it can drastically change the output of the photo.

Again, keep it simple and don't go over the top. Although these are just basic editing, going over the top with these adjustments can decrease the overall quality of the pictures. You don't want to lose its natural look. Always compare the edited output to the original pictures so you can easily tell whether or not you went overboard or you just did it right.

7. Consider Effects or Filters

The beauty of smartphone photo editing tools is that they come with preset filters that you can use with all pictures in order for them to have the same theme or aesthetics. Furthermore, it allows you to create very attractive photos without needing to be an expert.

You can draw the attention of your audience by adding creative filters and effects. Don't be afraid to try them all until you get the output you desire. But then again, try not to use filters to their full intensity. You can always adjust the settings of these filters in order to find the optimum level of outcome. And again, less is more.

8. It's Always the Quality over Quantity

One high-quality picture is worth more than 10 bad ones. If you think being active on Instagram by uploading consistently is more important than paying more attention to the quality of the picture you are uploading, then you have to know that you are doing things completely wrong! Keep in mind that it's better to spend hours taking a couple of good pictures than spending a few minutes taking hundreds of bad pictures.

9. Practice Makes Perfect

As cliché as it sounds, taking good pictures is skills that can be developed. And just like any other skills, it's something you can hardly achieve overnight. Practice. Don't be afraid to experiment and try not to get frustrated if you are not satisfied with the results you get on your first tries. Keep trying and before you know it, you will have thousands of followers waiting for your next upload.

In order to have the perfect photos for your Instagram business page, being a professional photographer or editor is not necessary. With the help of the tips and tricks above, you can end up with engaging and captivating content that can help you earn thousands of followers.

7.2 How to Create the Perfect Videos for Your Instagram Business Page

When it comes to editing videos, it sure sounds more intimidating for many compared to editing simple pictures. It's pretty understandable – after all, unlike a simple picture, a video consists of multiple frames that may have different lighting, contracts, and shadows. But what people didn't know is that it can be as simple as editing photos. You just have to make sure that you edit your videos matching your branding by adding texts, adjusting its brightness, and cropping it accordingly.

Today, adding videos for their business accounts is no longer only for big brands, any startup business can easily produce high-quality videos that can help them generate more engagement. You also don't need to spend a lot of money to hire a professional to do things for you. You can do it on your phone using free apps.

7.2.1 Tips to Creating the Perfect Picture

When we hear "Instagram aesthetic", the first thing that might come to your mind are attractive photos, professionally made presets, and appealing filters. But with the benefits Instagram video brings, it's important to make the most of it by applying this aesthetic to your videos as well.

It's amazing how there's no limit to what you can do with the videos you can upload on Instagram – main reasons why more and more people, whether the business account or not, are fond of using them.

Everything including Stories, GIFs, and Boomerangs are considered as video content on Instagram. This means that regardless of what type of multi-frame content you're posting, you want to make sure that you've got the right set of tools in creating high-quality video content for your Instagram.

Producing captivating videos for Instagram is one of the most efficient Instagram marketing tactics there are. Videos can be anywhere from 3 to 60 seconds long or longer if you want to upload the video on IGTV and could be uploaded straight from your phone, or by sending the files onto your phone from another source like a computer. This offers you a great amount of flexibility when it comes to using video content in improving your strategy for Instagram marketing.

Today, there's no denying to the fact that video content is the most shared type of content on the platform as it offers the brands an extremely appealing means to market as they tell more about the products. But then again, producing a share-worthy video on Instagram involves some efforts and brainstorming.

In this chapter, you will also learn some of the most practical and tactical ways to plan and shoot Instagram videos for better output and gather more views and engagement. You will also learn some of the examples of different types of Instagram videos you can try to make and upload.

Just like any other aspect of Instagram marketing campaigns, you will want to start the process of creating videos with a clear goal and a well-developed plan.

Setting Clear Goals

Telling a story in just 30 seconds can be a challenge for many. That's why taking your time in planning and conceptualizing a compelling video is extremely important. Before getting started, it's important to ask yourself what your main goals are for sharing the videos. Do you want to gain new followers? To make sales? Or maybe you want people to check out your website?

It's important to be specific. The feel and the tone of the video you are trying to create will depend on the reason as to why you are creating it in the first place.

Tell a Story

Creating a video that tells a story is the more effective way to gain attention and engagement on Instagram as a business. You don't have to make a storyboard for this, but by planning out the video well, you can assure that you will be able to use every second optimally. Doing this will help you manage your time properly and organize the storyline better.

You have to remember that Instagram videos start playing automatically when the user scrolls down their feeds, so it's important to start your video with an attention-grabbing scene. Starting your video this way is going to help it stand out, and more importantly, it's going to capture the interest of the viewer and convince them to watch the whole video to finish the story. But of course, the middle and the end parts of the video have to be strong as well.

At the end of the video, you may want to include call-to-action wherein you can ask the viewer to engage in the content or take action to learn more about your brand.

Lastly, you have to remember that videos on Instagram play in silent unless the user chooses to tap the video to enable the sound. So, you may also want to consider adding on-screen options.

Proper Lighting for Your Video

Just like when you are editing pictures, you don't need to invest in expensive lighting equipment in order to have fantastically well-lit video output. Choosing the settings is always the key, but using some basic technique can also help dramatically. Here are some tips to remember:

- **Use natural light sources.** As much as possible, shoot during the daytime when the sun is out and shining. And it's better if it's outdoors. However, if you're shooting indoors, try to shoot it near the windows and make sure to keep the light in front of you and shining in your direction.
- **Avoid shooting under overhead lights**. Doing this can cause some very poor visual effects. Seek other sources of light and help your subject is moving around until you get to find a good light source.
- **Use your creativity!** If ever your lighting setup isn't doing you any favor, this is when you have to wring your creative juice. If you want to soften the light, you can use a white poster board or even a simple paper to be your reflector. Similarly, if you're aiming to block some unwanted light source, you can use black plastic to cover it.

Shooting the video

Choosing what camera to use for shooting your video is the first thing you need to do. It's best to use the camera directly from your smartphone or DSLR instead of the camera function within the Instagram app. This is because the app's camera has some limitations when it comes to shooting capabilities.

After choosing the camera to use, the next step is shooting the video! Here are some pointers to help you as you start shooting your Instagram videos for your business.

- **Always shoot the video in portrait for Story or landscape mode for Feed**. Thankfully, it didn't take long before Instagram realized that cropping videos and photos into a square is not the best idea they came up with for the platform. This means you can decide as to what orientation you want to upload in. For uploading normal content, it's best to upload it in a landscape, while stories are best taken in portrait. This is because playing Stories will give you a full-screen view while a typical video on the feed doesn't do that. Setting the orientations these ways will give the users full views of the video while playing.
- **Keep the focus on the subject**. Make sure that the device you are using is consistently focusing on the subject. When using your smartphone to shoot the video, you can simply tap the screen on the area where you want it to focus. On the other hand, if you are using a DSLR, you might have to adjust the lens to get it focused on the subject.
- **Keep the shot steady**. Unless you are trying to shoot an indie or a horror film, you'll want to keep

the shot steady. You can use a tripod if you are shooting a video in the same frame. On the other hand, if you are shooting a video where you have to move, then you can use a stabilizer like a gyro device.

- **Be picky**. Depending on where you are planning to upload your video, it can be as short as 10 seconds up to 60 seconds or more if you're planning to upload it on IGTV, but then again, because there's a limit to how long you can play the video, you must be selective about what you will include in the video. When editing the video, ask yourself if the scenes you will include are worth being in the video.

Choosing the Content to Upload

There are some categories that will help you to decide on what type of content to upload. These categories include a brand image, types of products, and the story you want to portray in your video.

From there, you can start brainstorming. List down all the ideas you have relevant to the subject and format that you think will help you create a compelling video for your business. Lastly, you have to make sure that the content you make fits the theme and tone for your brand. Again, you must remember that consistency is a very important thing.

Below are different types of video content you can upload on your Instagram. Check the list carefully and find out which types of content you think is the one that will match your marketing goals.

Product details

Show your followers the products you are selling and why they should buy them. Uploading videos that show your products and their features a couple of times a week is ideal. Doing this will be a great complement to uploading lifestyle photos and videos. Uploading this type of videos will provide your followers with an insight into what your brand embodies.

Product-in-action

If you want to break up the monotonous series of staged images on your feed, uploading product-in-action videos would be a great solution. Your followers will not want to see a series of showroom stock photos on your feed.

When you are trying to determine what video to create for product-in-action, you must consider your audience and what gives them inspirations. What kind of customers to do they have and what do they really want? Put yourself in their shoes and look at your brand from a different point of view.

Sneak previews

Are you about to release a new product? If so, announce the news with a teaser video that gives your followers a sneak peek at the new product you're about to launch. By intensifying the hype and excitement surrounding your new release, you'll make your followers think, wonder, and daydream about your product before its even available.

Behind-the-scenes

Behind-the-scenes or BTS for short is video content that is good for building a more personal connection with your followers. When you introduce yourself and your team to your audience, you are giving them backdoor access to how you operate your brand. This will also give you an opportunity to communicate with your audience in an authentic way and generate an intimate connection with them.

Here are some of the themes you can consider uploading in your BTS video:

- **A day in the life**. This will show your followers what a typical day at work in your office looks like.

- **A tour within your office, warehouse, or studio.** Many of your followers are surely curious about what your work station looks like. Show them where you work.

- **Special events**. If you have a product launch or other company events, bring your followers backstage.

- **Staff introductions**. Introducing your followers to the staff and employees will surely give them a different level of trust in your brand knowing that you are more than willing to introduce the identity of the people working in the brand.

- **Work in action**. Show how you create the product and how you put up things together to come up with high-quality products that you are selling to them.

Tutorials

Entertain your followers by showing them how to use your product properly – not only entertaining but also instructive. You can also add humor to your video – people love it!

Series

If you are planning to upload videos that are more than one minute long, you can create a series that break up the whole thing in 60-minute segments. Uploading interesting video content will make your followers ask for more. This will help you gain new followers and more engagement.

Videos on loop

Known as Boomerang, Instagram now uses looping videos like what Vine had. This is when the video automatically starts and repeats in a loop. This is a good way to showcase a fun way to show your products and their features.

Consider using looping videos to showcase a fun or versatile product feature.

Stop motion videos

You need to use an editing app to create this kind of video. And to shoot this, you need to take individual photos of each frame using your camera. And with the help of a stop motion editing up, you can stitch the videos together to create great video content for your Instagram.

Time-lapse videos

This kind of video is popularly used when filming a scenery wherein there's a continuous movement. Most of today's smartphone offers this feature. However, if the phone or camera you are using doesn't have this feature, there are, of course, apps you can install in your phone to edit a video and turn it into a time-lapse one.

If you don't know already, time-lapse videos are condensed longer videos, this means filming a short time-lapse video will take a long time to do. Because of this, it's recommended to use a tripod to mount your camera with. If you're filming using your phone, you might want to set it into airplane mode to make sure that your filming wouldn't get interrupted by incoming calls and texts.

As you can see, you have several options when it comes to choosing the kind of video to upload on your business profile. But in order to come up with a compelling video for your marketing strategy, there are some important points you need to keep in mind: plan early, take your time and consider your followers' goals and lifestyles.

Conclusion

Instagram has officially become the next big thing. Many businesses have migrated to Instagram, mainly due to its better interface and user-friendliness. Aside from businesses migrating their business to this platform, many people also created an account with the sole intent of making money.

Today, being an influencer is seen as a career by many. While this is not fully accepted by some, there's no denying to the fact that, it's legitimately a good way to make a living.

If you have an Instagram account with a big following, you have a big chance of being successful in this platform. As soon as people you don't personally know starting liking, sharing, and tagging their friends in your posts, that's when you know you are doing the right thing. An Instagram profile can get viral, especially if it brings entertainment to people.

On the other hand, if you have a business that needs more exposure, Instagram is also a great platform to make your name big. When running a business, exposure is the key, and because everyone has an Instagram account now, you will have more opportunities to be seen.

With the methods, tips, and techniques mentioned in this book on how to earn money on Instagram, we hope that it will be easier for you to be successful in this making money with it. Again, remember the key elements of running an Instagram account – high-quality content, engagement, and dedication. Once you are able to execute these things together, you are on your way to success.